Now I Call Him Brother

Alec Smith

Marshalls

Marshalls Paperbacks
Marshall Morgan & Scott
3 Beggarwood Lane,
Basingstoke, Hants, RG23 7LP, UK

Copyright © 1984
Alec Smith and Rebecca de Saintonge
First published by Marshall Morgan & Scott Ltd.

Printed 11/84

ISBN 0 551 01079 7

Cover photo by Tim Leach.
Typeset by Performance Print Services Ltd.
11a Broughton Manor, Broughton, Milton Keynes
Printed in Great Britain by
Anchor Brendon Ltd., Tiptree, Colchester

Contents

1. A Quiet Beginning

I don't want to make any excuses. I'd have gone off the rails no matter who my father had been, there was just something in me, and I can't find it in my heart to blame him.

People think that because my father was Prime Minister we must have been quite a sophisticated family, but that really wasn't true. Even though politics have played such a dominant part in his life, Dad's first love is, and always has been, farming – and I was a typical farmer's son. I'd rattle around with him in his truck, help with the harvesting, feed the pigs, pick the tobacco and walk beside him in the evenings for the family's ritual stroll before sundown. For the first few years of my life I hardly left his side.

As kids we always knew he was in pain. He'd been an RAF pilot during the war and was shot down twice; the first time over the Western desert, and although he'd escaped, his face was a terrible mess and he had to have plastic surgery to reconstruct it.

The second time he was shot down in Italy and his legs were badly burnt and broken. Even so he fought for six months with the Italian partisans behind German lines before walking over the Alps to rejoin the allied forces. But his legs were never the same again and even in the height of summer Dad always wore long trousers. To us he was quite a hero.

The house, which my parents still live in, is a typical Rhodesian farmhouse; single storey with one room rambling off into another. It started off quite small, but bits have been added on here and there as the family expanded and finances improved. Like most African farmsteads it has a tin roof and a slightly scruffy veranda permanently netted to keep out the mosquitoes.

Mum never fussed about the house. We lived in a sort of homely shambles. We had a handful of watercolours which hung in clusters and faded quietly with the years. There were yards of books – the sittingroom is practically lined with them – and you could turn almost any corner and come across a clutter of toys and treasures that we'd been hoarding over the years; old cows' horns, guinea fowl feathers, bits of rock – the things kids always keep.

The farm itself is about 7000 acres set in the lowland hills of Selukwe. The land is mostly savanna – scrub land, very rocky, with a mass of low undergrowth and outcrops of boulders. Every square foot had to be cleared by hand before anything would grow. The trees were cut down, the roots dug up, the red soil sifted of rocks and stones. Around the house my parents planted tall flowering trees and in the distance we could see the mountainous hills of Longwe.

There was always a rhythm to our days, partly because of the heat. Dad was up and out by 6.30 and most of the hard work was done by half past ten when we'd gather on the veranda for a pot of tea and toasted buns. Dad, in his old farm shirt and long bags would talk quietly to the farm manager about the day's chores, the dogs lolling at his feet.

He kept pedigree pigs in the early days, with cattle and a few horses. As the land was cleared he planted tobacco and later superb mealies (that's our version of Maize – very pale and succulent!) which are the staple diet of Africa.

Because he was an MP he was away in Salisbury for several months of the year and my mother had to learn to cope on her own. I don't think many people realised quite what that meant for her. She was a highly intelligent and cultured lady used to a stimulating city life – music, theatre, entertaining. Her first husband had been a doctor and a well-known Rugby international and they'd enjoyed a good social life. One afternoon, when my sister Jean was a todler and brother Rob just a babe in arms, Mum had a phone call to say that her husband had been injured in a Rugby match. He'd broken his neck and died.

Now she found herself living in a remote farm-house, four miles from the nearest white neighbours and at least 10 from the nearest town. The one road out was frequently flooded during the rainy season so that she could spend days, even weeks, alone with us children and our handful of farm workers. It takes some courage to adjust to that kind of isolation.

Because my brother and sister were older than me I spent most of those early years with the African farm boys. We did everything together. They were fantastic at cracking the long stock whips, and although I practised, I could never do it as well as them.

Dad used to let us drive his huge ox and cart to pick up mealie stalks in the fields. We'd stand in the cart with our legs bent, holding the reins like Roman charioteers and whooping. But even though I spent most of the day playing with the African kids, it was another 20 years before I brought an African home for tea. The only Africans that ever set foot in our house when I was young were servants – the rest you left outside.

We were never a family to hunt. We had to kill the jackels and leopards that slaughtered the cattle and the wild pig and baboons that would strip the maize crop, but by and large Dad preferred the game to be seen, not shot. Yet when my brother Rob came home for the school holidays we'd go out together with our pellet guns, more for the fun of it than to hit anything. We'd try to sneak up on the lizards that lay basking on the stones. Their skins were splashed with all the colours of the rainbow. In the tall trees around the house the weaver birds would build their nests on the very tips of the branches so that they dipped and swayed in the slightest breeze. We used to watch them stripping the leaves off so the snakes couldn't sneak up on them unnoticed.

By midday the heat, especially in summer, would be scorching, and after lunch everything stopped; the whole household, guests and all, would quietly disperse. A heavy silence fell on the farmstead as the sun burned into what was left of our grass and the glossy starlings flashed brilliant from tree to tree. I used to watch them out of the window and wonder how long it would be before everyone woke up again.

During the summer months the cattle had to be rounded up every week or so to be dipped because of the tics which carry all sorts of diseases. The African boys and I used to scuttle round the outside of the herd as it strolled through the enclosure to the trough, poking the stragglers with our sticks and hopping out of the way when they rolled their eyes. The mothers gave their young ones a butt so they splashed into the dip. I didn't blame them for being nervous. It looked disgusting. Like liquid creosote. It must have tasted foul. I can still see them, swimming desperately along, struggling to keep their heads clear.

Every evening when Dad was home we would take the two dogs and go for a family stroll around the farm; along the red path through the tobacco fields to the little river, past the quiet evening cows and over the rocky, tree-stumped savanna. Home again we'd sit on the veranda with our 'sundowner' (orange juice for us kids) and watch the sunset streaming over Longwe. African sunsets are sudden and spectacular and night falls quickly into a deep blackness.

I really think those early years were quite idyllic for a child, but they came to an abrupt end when I was sent, most reluctantly, to boarding school. I was seven and kicked up a terrible fuss. But worse was to come!

In April 1964 Dad became Prime Minister of Rhodesia. On the day it was announced he and Mum came to visit my brother and me at school.

'Have you heard the news?' said Dad, and Rob, who only ever read the back page of the paper and was a rugger fanatic said, 'Yes Dad. Isn't it awful, we lost again.'

2. Ian Smith's Son

The sitting room of the Prime Minister's residence was so vast you could play tennis in it and every room was covered in thick pile carpets. Even the loo. I worked out one day that the three lounges in the public reception area of the residence could sit fifty six people at any one time without bringing in any extra chairs.

I was twelve when we moved in and it was like being locked into the toy department at Harrods. Outside the house there were all sorts of alarm systems that I liked to show off to my friends. Once or twice we got too close and in a matter of minutes the gardens were swarming with police cars. The record was actually ninety seconds which was very impressive considering the grounds alone were about nine acres. Needless to say my friends and I lay low and looked innocent until it was all over.

Perhaps the most prestigious toy for a young lad was the huge map in Dad's study which turned out to be a door which swung back to reveal the safe where all the state secrets were kept. When he'd gone out in the mornings we used to creep in with a stethoscope we'd got from school and try to work out the combination, but we never made it.

There were treasures everywhere, not like the treasures at home – these were the real McCoy. There were big pictures in gilt frames on loan from the National Gallery; priceless Chinese vases in glass cases and in the hall there was a huge grandfather clock that had been given to a previous Prime Minister by the British House of Commons.

We had five servants working in the house and five in the garden. One man did all the cooking, another all the laundry and the whole team of them worked like unobtrusive bits of machinery, functioning with the least possible fuss to see that our lives ran smoothly. It was like living in an hotel: you pressed a button for whatever you wanted, and along it came.

In the garden there was a tennis court and a swimming pool and an immaculate croquet lawn which my friends and I violated by playing our own version which was more like ice hockey.

But there was a section of the house portioned off for our private use and there you could lounge around and leave things lying about without the fear that some dignitary would be ushered in. We also had a small dining room where we could be 'just family', but we were rarely 'just family' and that was the trouble.

Dad would come back from work at about 6.30 and have a few moments to put his feet up and drink some squash – he rarely touched alcohol – and perhaps watch the evening news over supper. Then he'd go to his study or out to an official function. We hardly had time to say hello between his coming in and his going back to work.

Mum would have official lunches, endless cocktail parties and dinners and be forever opening this and launching that. She was always immaculately dressed and left a trace of perfume in the air to remind you that she had been in, even if you'd not been quick enough to catch her! All a far cry from the days when, sweaty and dusty, we'd curl our fingers round mugs of cocoa and look with satisfaction at a barn full of tobacco.

But it wasn't just at home that I noticed a change. Things started to go wrong at school. It happened so slowly at first that I hardly noticed it, but I began to realise that people had stopped calling me by my name. I had become 'Ian Smith's son'. No one introduced me as Alec. My name was lost. Boys I didn't particularly care for would sidle up and try to be friends and I could feel it was nothing to do with my personality but rather that I was the PM's son and there might be something in it for them. On the other hand many of those I counted on and liked fell away. One friend I was close to came straight out with it; 'I'm sorry Al, but my folks don't want me to visit you any more because they don't agree with your old man's politics.'

I couldn't believe it. What had Dad's politics got to do with me? I didn't even know what his politics were. I was terribly hurt and angry. Not with Dad. It wasn't his fault these guys were all so stupid, but I felt increasingly helpless in the face of such enforced anonymity. I had ceased to be Alec, I was just 'Ian Smith's son'. It was as if they were trying to wipe me out somehow.

It was at this stage that I began to enjoy getting drunk. I had already begun to smoke before Dad was PM and my interest in liquor was much more to do with devilment than despondency. I got a kick out of doing things that were not considered 'acceptable'. Our school was run on Eton and Harrow lines – all bloaters and grey flannel 'longs', busting at the seams with the sons of the rich, mostly farmers, and if you played good Rugby you were practically deified. Well my crowd didn't play good Rugby, by and large, and the only person we deified was Elvis Presley. Our real aim in life was to become Elvis clones and to this end we slicked our hair back and wore our trousers as tight as we could get away with.

We also brewed our own wine under the floor boards in the dormitory. We'd make it out of anything – mulberries, oranges, whatever was going. Unfortunately one day it blew up. We came back from lessons to find the whole place stinking like a brewery and the matron still in a state of shock. She had thought it was an earthquake.

But we'd drink anything we could get hold of and one of our crowd, a real screwball called Johnny, used to nick methadryn tablets from a local chemist.

It was a much coveted drug because we found we could take five or six tablets on a Friday night and that would give us enough zip to party all weekend.

I really enjoyed getting drunk. I enjoyed the changes of perception that getting drunk gave you. It made me happy. I wasn't conscious of being unhappy when sober – on the contrary, life was pretty good – but being drunk just felt even better.

Not surprisingly I passed only two O levels the first time around. I was sent to the school psychologist who gave me an IQ test that registered 165, which blew my gaff, and it was decided that I should live at home in the official residence and become a day scholar. Maybe my work and lifestyle would take a turn for the better under the discipline of the parental eyes. The trouble was that the parental eyes were glued firmly on the things of state and for the next few years they hardly saw me at all.

My brother and sister were both at University by this time and I was left to struggle alone through the interminable state dinners. For me food has always been something you eat, simply and quickly, in order to get on with the next thing. I found it excruciating to have to stand through endless meaningless chat over the sherry glasses and then to plough laboriously through course after course, coffee and liqueurs, especially as I was nearly always saddled with the most boring of the guests with whom, being at least forty years my senior, I had nothing whatsoever in common.

After a while I began to excuse myself from the formal dinners and ate my own meals in the kitchen. I used the back door to come and go and kept my own time and my own company. The house was so huge and my parents so busy that I could literally not see them for two or three days on end, which suited me fine. I shall always remember one afternoon when I bumped into a couple of school friends in town who had nowhere to stay. 'Come back with me', I said, 'we've got plenty of bedrooms'. It was two days before my mother even knew they were there, despite the fact that they'd eaten breakfast, lunch and dinner with us.

I never bragged about the fact that Dad was Prime Minister, but it did enable me to offer my friends a slightly more exotic form of entertainment than we might otherwise have been able to afford. I can still recall the weekend they went away and left me in sole possession of the Residency. I decided to hold a party and invited everyone I could think of, including the police who patrolled the grounds.

People wandered all over the house, played sport, got drunk, knocked about the swimming pool. The stereo blasted away playing the Moody Blues and the Rolling Stones and the party lasted the whole weekend. One friend brought his hot rod – an old Austin A90 with a huge engine in it – and spent the better part of the day using our immaculate driveway as a drag strip. It was two years before the marks began to fade.

In the end the neighbours complained, which was fair enough, but quite something when you realise that our closest neighbours were nearly a quarter of a mile away! The Residence is surrounded by a polo ground, a golf course, an agricultural experimental farm and, on the fourth side, woodlands and gardens which lead to Government House.

News of the party spread all over town and I had some explaining to do when my parents eventually got home.

By the time the 'swinging sixties' had reached Africa they were almost on the way out, but I was ready and waiting for them. I'd been sent to a crammer in Bulawayo run by a crazy Australian called Digger Wells. Digger was a brilliant teacher with a reputation for being able to handle difficult kids. He viewed our flowing hair and strings of beads with the equanimity of a man who has come to terms with the fact that nothing he says will stop a lemming hell-bent for the sea. He was more than willing to get us through exams if that's what we wanted, but on the other hand, he was quite happy to bail us out of the pub when the necessity arose – even though we were under age – provided we did the same for him. Which we did. Quite often. So Digger drank and we drank – and smoked and popped whatever pills were available.

My parents, embroiled as they were in more important things, hadn't the faintest clue what was going on until one evening, when they had an agitated phone call from my aunt.

It was a Saturday and a group of us kids had picked huge bunches of flowers from the municipal flowerbeds and were distributing them with benedictions of 'love and peace' to the bewildered morning shoppers. Bulawayo is, and always was, a most conservative community. It didn't know what to make of us. This particular Saturday about thirty of us gathered for a Love-In in the park. One guy, dressed up as a high priest, conducted a wedding while the rest of us sat around smiling and kissing and jingling little bells. Finally the local TV station caught up with us and invited us in to the musical chat show to explain what we were about – and I was the spokesman.

My aunt Joan was at home, knitting in front of the telly and thinking idle thoughts like, 'these disgusting young hippies', when she suddenly heard a voice she recognised. Looking up from her knit one purl one she got the shock of her life! She rushed to phone my folks who completely freaked out.

I was flown home for a talking to. It had all come as a terrible shock to them and I remember Dad's eyes positively glittering; 'Alec', he said, his voice clipped with parental outrage, 'Get those beads off and wash your hair. When you're decent I'll speak to you.'

Poor Dad, worse was to come. But Digger? He didn't give a damn. 'Boys will be boys' he said.

Somehow I got my 'A' levels and it was decided that I should read law. I'd always fancied myself as a debator and I had a sort of Perry Mason image of what a lawyer did. It all seemed rather fun. So I enrolled at the University of Rhodes, South Africa, and off I went.

3. The Happy Hippie

For most of my friends the sixties were a turbulent time. It was the heyday of 'relativism' and it knocked a hole in many of their lives.

As students we were introdced to a whole range of political theorists from Plato and Aristotle down to Chairman Mao. We were taught to look at the way religions had been used to manipulate societies and we analysed the behaviour of religious groups in a style that was both scathing and destructive. Under the scrutiny of the sociologists all sense of the spiritual disappeared. So also did any clear cut views of morality. Truths that we had been brought up to believe inviolate were proved to be only relative. They, and we, were simply the products of our environment; our parents, our society, our century. Had we been brought up in some other country, at some other time, in some other way, our system of values might have been completely different and just as valid. In other words, there was no such thing as absolute truth. Everything was relative.

As the moral and spiritual foundations were kicked from beneath their feet, many of my friends felt they had nothing to hold on to any more. They couldn't locate themselves. They felt abandoned in some strange way, and bitterly disillusioned. Their world of values had been turned upside down and declared a nonsense.

It was one thing to rebel against the conventional attitudes to dress and sex, which most of us were, but when all that you believe in as moral and true is shattered, and when it's clearly demonstrated to you that, in a case, there are no truths to be found, then that's another ball game.

For many of my friends, God went out the window and in his place there flooded a sense of hopelessness and helplessness. The world had been turned inside out. To hell with everyone then. It was each man for himself.

So it was with a genuine and rather desperate longing that many of my generation turned to drugs. We had a sort of hazy vision of a new world where all the aggro that separated man from man would be eradicated; where race and class and culture would no longer be a barrier to human loving. We tripped away, partly in rebellion, partly in despair.

For me, however, things were made a little easier because, by and large, I refused to think at all. I would not let myself despair. If things got a bit heavy, I just smoked another joint. I sat on the fringes of political and spiritual conversations, but I was really out for fun, and fun was drugs.

Hash was our staple diet. Every night I'd roll a joint and leave it on the table by my bed so that first thing when I woke I could just stretch out and light it. That gave me enough energy to get out of bed. Morning lectures would have come and gone by that time, but if I pushed myself I could get to the canteen before lunch. But I soon graduated to LSD and my one motivation in life became the next trip. Who cared about the lectures anyway? Give me the botanical gardens with their widespreading trees sprawling with luscious purple bougainvillea. I could learn far more out there, tripping with my mates in the shade, than I could ever learn in the lecture hall. I passed my first lot of exams by swotting up the crib notes to the set books and picking the brains of a few friends the day before. Nothing else seemed necessary.

During the vacs my friends and I returned home to Rhodesia where our lifestyle continued without interruption. Salisbury must be one of the loveliest cities in Africa. According to tradition the streets had been built wide enough to turn an ox cart – and that's pretty wide – and on either side the walkways are lined with a rash of garishly flowering trees. Trees grow tall very quickly in Africa and their flowers are large and waxy, the colours clashing orange, pink and red in a crazy cascade. They look like birthday cakes that have been lavishly decorated by someone who didn't know when to stop.

Every season has its speciality. In November the Red Flamboyants explode into flower and the Flame trees burst out like huge orange horse chestnuts, while the summer jacarandas, their flowers the colour and texture of wisteria, form a massive purple dome over the city traffic. In the first rains they drop and the pavements and verges shimmer like a bluebell wood. We always tell our visitors to listen for the pop-pop-pop of the flower buds as the cars and cycles ride over them.

The residential houses are nearly all bungalows set in an acre of land. Thick hibiscus hedges surround the gardens and the air on a hot afternoon is heavy with scent. It's more like some exotic garden suburb than a capital city – at least where the whites live it is. There's nothing but red dust and mealies in the black townships, but then, they weren't built for pleasue.

But amid all this cultivation there are still pockets of unspoiled land and my friends and I knew every hidden copse or stretch of bush where it was possible to smoke undetected. Sometimes we'd sit right out in the open, lolling in the shade of a little thorn tree. The bush was so flat and bare that we could see anyone coming from some way off and we didn't think our little bit of smoke would be noticed in the general heat haze of mid morning. But our favourite place was a patch of eucalyptus trees not far from the centre of town which we called The Magic Forest. It was in quite a built up area, but they'd left this little pocket of cultivation untouched. We had to push our way through waist high undergrowth until we came towards the trickle of a stream. A huge tree had fallen across the water like a bridge and here we'd get as high as kites, amusing ourselves in a fantasy world of hobbits and high wizardry.

As my friends were quick to point out, I was not really interested in politics (I had a picture of Che Guevara on my wall, but I preferred the one of

Jimmi Hendrix), but in my more energised moments – and they were few – I joined in the activities of the National Union of South African Students, NUSAS. They were a radical, revolutionary body that frightened the government stiff. The things we spoke out against – like apartheid and lack of academic freedom for the blacks – would have been accepted without question in Europe, but in South Africa we were considered 'a threat to state security'. We were continually scrutinized by the security forces who were trying to establish links between us and banned organisations like the African National Council and the Communist Party. The press were quick to pick up my own association with NUSAS and I enjoyed the publicity.

I became a spokesman for student activism. I joined street demonstrations for black rights and spoke out in public against the South African government. In fact we were the forerunners of an explosive student movement that was to spread across South Africa ending in mass rioting on the campuses and the police turning out with tear gas and truncheons. The riots made headlines all over the world.

But I wanted to go still further than NUSAS. I wanted to become even more extreme, to push the barriers of personal rebellion back still further, and so a group of us got together and formed the Rhodes SDS – Students for a Democratic Society. We didn't just want to challenge the authorities, we wanted to offend them. I mean really offend. We were pre-punk punk politicians. We were out to shock and the methods we used were vile – though I can't think now why we thought vomit more persuasive than argument.

Yet despite the fact that I appeared to be fighting

for black freedom, I wasn't really that committed. You see there were in the 'counter-culture revolution' two distinct groups, the Yippies, who were a minority really committed to social change, and the Hippies, who were primarily out for a good time. For us, political demonstrations were just something we did, like smoking pot. It was part of a general protest against the status quo.

The truth is that black freedom didn't really mean anything to me personally. What did mean something to me personally was standing up and being identified as a spokesman for a radical, anti-authority, anti-establishment group. It was a boost to the image I was so carefully creating. It meant a lot to me to hear someone say, 'Hey, see that guy over there? He's a real screwball.' Everyone knew I was degenerate. It didn't lower my status in their eyes one bit, on the contrary, and I'd rather have been known as a degenerate any day, than as Ian Smith's son.

The press were, of course, always quick to pick up my involvement with extreme political groups and there's no doubt that this finally contributed to my being sent down at the end of the first year. I was, as Ian Smith's son, an acute embarrassment to an already embarrassed South African parliament, and Dad wasn't too happy either. I also flunked my end of term exams. I rolled up in my dirtiest blue jeans, a torn tea-shirt with a red fist – the symbol of the SDS – sprayed on the front in red paint, and reeking of alcohol and grass. I arrived ten minutes late and wrote what at the time I thought a hugely funny answer to the Latin question: 'The works of Justinian', I scrawled, not focusing too clearly on the page, 'have been translated by far more emenant Latin scholars than I will ever be. I suggest you refer to them for my answer.' And with a final flourish, I left. Never to return again, as it turned out.

So at 21 I had acquired a reputation as a political extremist and a drop-out. I was already well on the way to becoming hooked on LSD and had tried almost everything else as well. I had virtually severed contact with Mum and Dad but I felt safe at last among a crowd I knew accepted me for myself and who were as embarrassed about my parents as I was. But love was not a part of my life, nor hope, nor vision. I lived entirely for my own pleasure.

4. The Seeds of Hatred

Because of my University course I was exempt from national service for five years, but when I returned home, there were my call-up papers waiting for me. It was quite clear to me that Dad had put pressure on the authorities to call me up so that they could 'clean up' his hippie son. I was furious.

I wrote to the exemption board explaining I was still a registered student but no go. These guys had been told to get me and get me they would. Not many people contradicted my father in those days.

But it was unthinkable. I was a peace-loving child of the sixties. How could I get trussed up in any army uniform with a gun and go around learning to shoot people? If I couldn't get out of it by fair means, I'd get out by foul. I called on a friend in the medical faculty and asked him to put me on drugs that would so louse up my medical they'd have to reject me as unfit. I can't remember now what I took, I only know that I felt like a zombie. The doctor failed to get any response from my reflexes or my blood pressure, which was so low by the time I had my test that he couldn't even get it to register. Imagine my amazement when he pronounced me fit! I felt physically lousy, but psychologically worse. Sitting in that doctor's room I began to experience the first real hatred of my father. It was as though I could never escape him, never shake him off my back.

That whole spell in the army was like a bad trip, a perpetual nightmare – from the first few hours when you are literally stripped and shorn, not only of your clothes and hair, but of your personality, of everything you recognise as you – right through to the final dismissal. It was as if once you'd signed on the dotted line and stepped into uniform you became a part of a machine with as much say over your life as the wheel of a car.

My first impression during the initial days was of everyone shouting and swearing at me, of a sort of mindless aggression for which I was the butt, and I was frightened. I was frightened that the system could have so much power over me. The army is a total experience and there is not the tiniest corner of your life that it doesn't take over, and take over with a brutality that is literally shocking. I couldn't believe that my own father could do this to me, that he could allow me to be violated in this way. And it was, in a sense, the second time that his position as PM had stripped me of my right to be myself.

I remember clearly that when I was in the reception area, just signing in, one of the officers whispered in my ear, 'You're Smith, aren't you? Make no mistake, we're going to get you.' I realised then that I'd been sent to the Army to get 'straightened out', and I vowed to myself that I would never, never reform. However much I was humiliated, I would not be forcibly changed.

The first six months they make particularly hard. Most people in Africa will get up at about half five or six in the morning, but in the army we had to get up every day between three and four o'clock in order to clean the barrack room. They were fanatical. If any housewife had kept her home so clean she'd have been sent to the psychiatrist, but in the army it was just a way of breaking you down. The big inspection was on Friday mornings. At eight o'clock sharp the commanding officer, who was a mean guy with electric blue eyes, would walk into the barrack room while we stood there in stiff silence. You could tell he was not at all interested in what you had cleaned, only in some remote and inaccessable part he thought you might not have cleaned. He'd prowl about, his eyes flickering round the room with what I always thought was childishly malicious delight. It was really pathetic that grown men could play such stupid games, but it must have given him a great sense of power over us. And we were in his power. If his hairy little finger found a trace of dust on a window ledge or on the castors of a bed, the whole bunch of us would be confined to barracks for the weekend, all our passes cancelled, our one contact with the outside world severed.

It was during one of these inspections that they discovered my socks. Socks in themselves would have been bad enough, but these socks, hidden in the rafters above my bed, were stuffed to the ankles with marijuana! I had only been in the army six weeks and I was actually in hospital at the time having been injured in weapon training. That was to be my saving. I think one of the straight guys told the Commanding Officer where it was, but anyway, first thing I knew was when the army police strode into the hospital ward, full of self-importance, as if they were about to arrest a long hunted war criminal.

'Smith', said the short one with the protruding pectorals, 'Get your shoes on. The Commanding Officer wants to see you. Now.' I was marched through the ward, and I remember the other guys looking up from their books and cards with a sort of cagey sympathy. No one likes to see a guy marched off by the police. Too many had returned the worse for wear.

I was jack booted across the tarmac and into the officer's building. The small guy with the pushed out chest knocked sharply on the door. 'Enter', roared a voice. It was like a third rate war film. My apprehension, however, was first rate. And when I walked in the room and saw my socks on the Officer's desk and the Officer himself looking like he'd just won a million pounds on the pools, my heart plummeted.

I didn't really take in what the guy said, my head was too full of all the stories I'd heard about Military Prison. Drug taking was a serious offence in the army and there was no doubt in my mind, or in the mind of the Commanding Officer, that the Military Court would sentence me to a spell inside. My fears were particularly potent because only six months before two guys had died in detention because of the severity of their treatment.

All armies throughout the world are famous for the crass forms of punishment they think up. In our Army they were legally allowed to push you to the limits of your physical strength, three times a day.

That means they could push you to the point of collapse — usually by making you carry something like a sack of bricks on your back and forcing you to run round and round in circles. When you fell down they'd chuck cold water over you, get you up, and make you run until you dropped again. This could happen three times in twenty four hours for 28 successive days. The trouble was that a few months before they'd done it to a young guy who had an unsuspected heart condition and he'd dropped dead. The other soldier was being put through a similar routine when he complained of acute stomach pains. They refused to believe him and eight hours later he died of a burst appendix.

So with these stories still fresh in my mind, I was less than anxious to go to Military Prison. Even if you did come out alive, which of course most people did, you never came out the same.

I stood to attention in that stuffy office saying 'Yes Sir', 'No Sir' — whatever seemed appropriate — until I was finally dismissed to await trial. What he actually said I don't know, but the gist of it was, 'We've got you this time, Smith'.

You really stand no chance in a military court. They assume that the fact that you've been brought so far means you're guilty. If you appeal against your sentence you get sent to a higher court, and a higher court has greater powers of punishment, so if they too find you guilty — and of course it's assumed that you are — then the punishment you get on appeal is greater than the original punishment. This knowledge acts as a firm deterrent against appeals, and only a madman would question his first sentence.

There is also a lot of boring paraphernalia

designed to humiliate you. You have to dress up in your best uniform which they then ceremonially strip off you, and I can remember the look of fat complacence on the C.O.s face as he relished the prospect of Smith being made to race round and round the block with a sack of bricks.

Happily for me it didn't happen that way. The hospital doctor was a decent man and he had no stomach for the methods used in the prison section. Nor was he prepared to take a risk on a soldier who appeared to have the health record I had, and who had just been wounded.

To the C.O.s disgust I was fined and confined to barracks for six weeks. I almost fell over with relief. I'd been even more frightened of the prison that I'd cared to admit. So in a sense, I won that round. It was to be the first win of many, but in future I was much more careful about the way I fought my personal war. I wasn't prepared to expose myself to so much danger again.

It was quite clear that open rebellion wouldn't work in the army, so I worked out a more subtle plan for survival. On the surface I appeared to knuckle down to the soldier's life – and I even became quite good at it – but underneath I was always scheming, finding ways of breaking the rules and scoring against the authorities. I wangled many a weekend off that I wasn't entitled to and took great delight in getting as stoned as a crow with all my mates. They were very faithful to me and had the parties all lined up for my weekends off. They also supplied me with pills and even grass, so that while my intake of drugs was reduced in the army, I was never completely without. I don't think a day passed when I wasn't able to take something.

But the feelings of bitterness against my father festered in me. I brooded a lot. Everyone was trying to change me. They rejected me for who I was and tried to bully or browbeat me into a different shape — the university authorities, my parents, and now the army. But I was determined that I was not going to change.

Actually I changed all the time, but not in the direction that everyone hoped for. Instead I got worse, more entrenched, and the resentment, anger and even hatred that I felt for my parents was building up in my heart.

I was demobbed from the army barracks in Bulawayo exactly nine months after the first initial hair cut. The last of my papers were signed and I got into my car and drove out through the gates like a bat out of hell. I heard them boom shut behind me and it was like suddenly waking up from the worst nightmare you've ever had. I drove 200 yards down the road and fell out of my tree. All of a sudden I just burst out laughing. It was delirious laughter, not funny laughter. I couldn't stop. I pulled up by the side of the road and the tears ran down my face.

From then on, of course, it had to be downhill. I had not the faintest shred of idealism or ambition left. I felt empty inside. I just couldn't drag up the motivation to go back to university. My one and only thought was to get back to the security of my friends and 'recover'. By recover of course I meant get stoned, for as long as possible, just to obliterate the memories of that terrible year. It had been the final wedge between my parents and myself. The whole army experience had been so totally negative and devastating that I never wanted to forgive them for it.

5. Escape Into Drugs

At this stage in my life God didn't come into my thinking at all. The only vaguely religious thing I had dabbled in, up till then, was Yoga, and then only because a mate of mine had told me it was a good way of getting high. He claimed all sorts of weird and wonderful things – that he'd levitated and floated around on his umbilical cord – I wasn't too sure I wanted to float around on my umbilical cord but what did appeal to me was his assurance that you could get as high on meditation as you could on drugs, but absolutely free of charge! That did sound good. The only trouble is that when you smoke a lot, as I did, you get very tired, so most of the time I just fell asleep, and never got round to meditating at all!

But when I came out of the army, my status as a hippie once more established, I started to go to some discussions at an Ashram in town. It was led by a very wise old sage called Swami Gi. He looked the part – sparkling eyes, a long orange robe and a lovely white beard. And there was something irresistible about him. He was obviously genuine and you felt that if only you could find what he'd found, you'd get the answer to whatever it was you were looking for, even if you weren't quite sure what it was. With most of my mind I was still looking for an answer to getting high without actual drugs, but part of me was interested in their claims that you could 'plug in to the source of eternal wisdom'. 'We can teach you to tune in to the river of life', they said, and I must say it sounded very alluring.

It was made all the more so because taking acid is in itself an extraordinary experience. You do really feel sometimes that you're at one with the universe, communicating with God, side by side with creation. It becomes a deeply mystical experience and some of my friends who were seriously seeking an expansion of reality would use LSD as a short cut to meditation, which must have made many an honest yogi roll in his grave.

I soon discovered that I could reach what I thought the Ashram was on about, without meditation, though I must admit that my experiences tended to be more freaky than spiritual. Perhaps the nearest we ever came to madness was when a group of us discovered mental telepathy. It later became something we sought after, though I still remember with some fear, the first time we came upon it unawares.

We were sitting in a group, four or five of us, pushing ourselves to get higher and higher. Suddenly I realised that we'd been talking for half an hour but none of us had said a word. We all became aware that we were hearing one another think. It was alarming because you couldn't have any secrets. I remember struggling to keep a tight grip on my thoughts. I felt everyone else would be able to read everything about me and I wasn't ready to bear my soul. It got worse. Emotions and feelings that my normal mind had buried in my subconscious because they were too difficult to handle, suddenly began bubbling to the surface. Long buried agonies and guilts became not only real to me but, I was sure, visible to everyone else as well. It was a horrible and terrifying experience.

I looked into the chemical causes of it all later and found that the human mind is capable of all sorts of perceptions but that our senses have evolved to block some out – otherwise we'd be overwhelmed with input. What LSD does is to lift that inhibition so that we become bombarded.

Your brain also has mechanisms for blocking out things it doesn't like, or doesn't want, and these too are lifted. That's when the lid comes off. You begin to have thoughts and fancies you would normally suppress and people who, when sober, would be hard pushed to climb a step-ladder – jump out of ten storey windows convinced they can fly.

Some of my friends did go mad. It was as though they just flipped and went somewhere else. You never really knew them again after that.

But I was hooked. I craved for the next trip. If I didn't get another within a couple of days, I'd suffer physical withdrawal symptoms and become nervy and on edge. But I wasn't worried. I wanted to be hooked. Drugs were the only meaningful thing in my life. They seemed so much more important than everything else because, compared with those extraordinary experiences, the rest of my life – family, friends, work – seemed so bland and dull, so totally uninteresting.

I made money by pushing. I dealt mostly in grass from Mozambique and LSD, which I smuggled in from Britain. I wasn't in the big time, I was just keeping myself going and tripping three or four times a week. I looked on myself as a sort of community service, providing people with the things they needed, that's all.

Of course we had some scary moments with the

police whom I came to hate with an almost paranoid hatred. They became The Enemy, and sometimes, on a bad trip, I would feel so terrified that we were going to be busted that I almost felt I was losing my mind. The drugs blew up the anxiety out of all proportion.

The grass I collected myself, but the LSD we had sent to us from the UK, smuggling it over in airmail letters. We had contacts in London who would mix the LSD in a liquid. In those days we used to take our LSD by putting a drop onto a sugar cube with an eye-dropper. The amount you take for each trip is microscopic, so that is the best way of doing it.

Our contact in London would mix it up. Then he'd get a piece of blotting paper the size of an ordinary sheet of writing paper and put 50 to 100 drops of LSD mixture – which of course was colourless – onto the paper at regular intervals. This was then sent through the post, and if anyone opened it who shouldn't, they'd just think you'd sent your blotting paper by mistake. I'd then cut the paper up into squares – about the size of a thumbnail – and they'd be ready to eat. I'd buy a trip from London for £1 and sell it in Salisbury for a fiver, so that wasn't too bad.

There was always the risk of the mail getting intercepted, but we took precautions. We'd usually get the stuff sent to a fictitious name – like John Smith – at our own address, and if the cops discovered it you'd say, 'I don't know this guy. I don't know why he's using my address'. And there was nothing they could do about it. That way we'd smuggle over 50 – 100 trips once or twice a week.

But we never pushed drugs to people who weren't

already users and there was a kind of morality amongst us.

We all knew how much they cost and it was accepted that the guy who took the risks was entitled to a few bucks for his trouble, but we didn't rip each other off. It was a much more supportive regime than that and we had a sense of fellowship, us against the rest of the world.

And that's how it went on for a couple of years.

6. Caught

One day not long before Christmas some friends and I were on our way back from Mozambique with a particularly good haul of grass. It was some of the best marujuana you could get. The trouble was that my rational judgement, never a strong point, was by now impaired by the quantity of drugs I was on, and I had been smuggling across the border for so long that I was getting slap happy about the whole thing.

So the first mistake I made was to travel back by bus. In those days only the Africans travelled by bus so a bunch of white honkies were extremely conspicuous. Everyone was looking at us before we'd even started. The second mistake was to climb onto the roof. African buses have huge roof-racks on which all the luggage is stowed – anything from suitcases and bicycles to chickens and second-hand refrigerators. They look like travelling junk shops and have an air of gay abandon about them. Maybe it was infectious, but anyway, when the bus made its scheduled stop at Tete I thought I'd better stow my hash somewhere safe before we crossed the border. Climbing the ladder to the roof I picked my way over the mound of luggage to find a safe spot to conceal it.

There was about 7 oz. of it which were wrapped up in banana leaves to look like corn cobs. I didn't think anyone would take much notice of them. But they did of me. A white man staggering all over an African bus in the centre of town is conspicuous enough, but a white man staggering all over an African bus in the centre of town and smoking a reefer is even worse. I eventually stuck the grass under the spare wheel and flopped down.

As soon as we got to the border I was arrested. The border guards found the hash immediately, doubtless tipped off by the bus conductor. My friends and I were carted off, loose legged and squealing, by the local police.

The interviews in Salisbury police station were like a classic cops and robbers. There was me sitting in a chair, demanding to see my lawyer and denying everything – even though I reeked of maru-juana – while one cop was pretending to be kind and the other tough in the hope that they could either lure or bully me into a simple confession. The truth was they'd known about me for some time but never been able to nail me before. Now they had me and I hadn't a leg to stand on. I was let out on bail to await trial.

I had a very good lawyer. We wrote the script together – he rehearsing me as vigorously as if we'd been opening on Broadway. He also insisted that I turn up sober – in every sense of the word.

The actual court appearance was a charade. I had

my hair cut for the occasion, wore a suit and club tie and looked the epitomy of contrite respectability. Neither Mum nor Dad turned up, but Mum wrote a nice letter saying I was 'artistic and idealistic' and she was sure I'd prove my worth as an industrious and useful citizen.

Det. Inspector D.J. Looker plodded through his 'on the afternoon of December 20th' and produced my cobs of hashish, which I remember looking at with great longing and wondering how I could get back. However I swore I was a light smoker and had only started for fun at University. The magistrate, Mr. Gerald Rose, said he found me genuinely penitent and determined not to smoke again. In view of which he wouldn't send me to jail. Instead I was fined 250 Rhodesian dollars (about £150) and had a six month suspended sentence. It could have been a lot worse.

As I left the court my friends were waiting. They whirled around me and whisked me away in their car. There was great jubilation as we roared away – and a fresh joint in my hand before we'd even turned the corner.

The press didn't actually pick it up until I appeared in court, and then the story hit the headlines all over the world; 'Smith's son smuggles Hashish'. 'Premier's son on drugs Charge'. It appeared in the New York Times, most of the British press, and I was sent cuttings from as far afield as Los Angeles, Canada and New Zealand.

So that was that. Blown. For my parents the whole episode was highly embarrassing. They knew my life style was pretty wild, but they hadn't realized quite how off the beaten track I'd gone. I know now that they never stopped loving me, but I was completely ostracised by their society and friends. Even some of my relatives cut me off without a word or a sign. It was as though I had never existed. 'It's your choice', I thought, and turned my back becoming, if that were possible, even more alienated from them all than ever before.

A friend's father got me a job in a photographic business – something I'd always been interested in – and I set about paying off my fine and trying to hold down a job while tripping at the same time. That needed some skill.

7. The Rocky Road to Christ

While my family and friends were busy erasing me from their memory, two groups of women – strangers – began to pray for me. One group was in America and the other in South Africa. They didn't know anything about me except what they had read in the papers, but for some reason they took it upon themselves to pray for me each week. I didn't know anything about it at the time, of course, and I wouldn't have been too impressed if I had, but looking back I can see with absolute clarity that it was at about this time that God began to interfere with my life.

There were all sorts of threads that led me to think about Jesus Christ in a serious way. One was the show, 'Jesus Christ, Superstar'. I remember being fascinated by it. It introduced me to Jesus as an identifiable person, and I'd never thought of him like that before. He wasn't the Jesus of the High

Anglican Church – shrouded in robes and incence and unattainability – on the contrary. This Jesus was a man who could be represented in pop music, he was part counter-revolutionary, part mystic. There were all sorts of elements in his personality I found I could relate to. I almost felt I had something in common with Jesus.

A lot of Christians have told me subsequently that they found the musical offensive, but all I can say is that for me it was a stepping stone.

I realised for the first time that Jesus did not represent the status quo. He hadn't fitted into people's image of what he 'should' be like. He'd been a rebel, like me, and I could relate to that.

Later there was 'Godspell', which was a jazzing up of St. Matthew's Gospel. This too I found very moving. I loved the music, and here were all these guys dressed just like my friends and I were – long hair, jeans, flowers – and they were all talking about Jesus. I felt Jesus must, somehow, belong to our crowd.

Another thing that occurred to me at this time was that often, when I went to the Ashram to hear Swami Gi, he would talk about the New Testament and Jesus Christ. It made me think that maybe there was enlightenment to be found in Western faith after all.

Even so I wasn't consciously searching for God. I was still living for drugs, even though I'd modified my intake so I could work; but my life still revolved completely around myself. When a close friend of mine told me he'd met Jesus on an acid trip, I thought he was fairly quaint, though even I could see his conversion was real enough. But I didn't envy him.

And then one evening a most extraordinary thing happened. I had been tripping in one of my favourite spots. In those days I cut down my smoking to the minimum during the day and saved the best trip for the way home when I'd go up to my favourite hill and watch the sunset. African sunsets are sudden and beautiful, but they're even more beautiful when aided by a little Malawi grass.

This evening I was driving home, high of course, when I heard a voice apparently coming from the back seat of my car. The voice said, 'Go home and read the New Testament'. I nearly jumped out of my skin. Someone must have sneaked in while I was smoking. I darted a look at the mirror. No one. I jammed on the brakes and pulled into the side. I was trembling and could hardly grip the handbrake. It was the shock of finding someone sitting behind you when you hadn't even suspected their presence. I whirled round in my seat to confront them. There was no one there. I found myself looking all round the car as if I'd lost a penny or something; I just couldn't believe it was empty. I was totally confused, but of one thing I was quite sure, that voice had not been an hallucination. It had been real, and in my heart of hearts I knew whose voice it was.

I didn't rush home to find a bible. I drove around, trying to put that clear voice out of my mind. But I couldn't. It kept nagging me. For two days I tried to forget it, to find some explanation for what it could have been, but the fact is I knew the voice in my car had been the voice of God himself, and I knew he was speaking to me. One evening I found I couldn't hold out any longer and going home I was determined to find a New Testament.

The very last thing you'd expect a bloke like me to

have is a bible. I hadn't read the bible since I was a little kid, and it had never meant anything to me then. But when I got home I opened my top drawer and there, looking at me, was the Gideon's New Testament that I'd been given at school more than 10 years before. To this day I don't know how it got there. I must have carted it all through my crammer and university days, right through the army and from pillar to post as I lived the life of a junkie, but I had no recollection of it at all during that time.

But this night, the first drawer I opened, there it was.

I began at St. Matthew's Gospel. I realised I must have read it before because bits of it were vaguely familiar, but this time it was as if I was reading it all for the first time. I'd never really understood it before, but now it was like a wonderful new revelation. I couldn't put it down. I picked it up at every spare minute and within a couple of days I'd worked right the way through to Revelation.

A rather curious side effect to all this was that the book itself was giving me physical hallucinations. I was smoking very moderately at the time and knew I wasn't high, but I remember looking at the bible and the whole thing seemed to be breathing, pulsating in my hand and the words were shining off the page and almost leaping into my mind. I remember thinking, 'this book is actually alive'.

A couple of weeks later a guy called Neil Gibbs, who worked down the road in a litho printing firm, asked me to go to his church with him. Now this fascinated me, partly because he didn't know me from Adam, he only knew me as the young photographer from the next block, and partly because no one had ever invited me to a church before. I'd been bullied into going, but never invited. And my interest was aroused not only by what I had been reading, but by the fact that the church he went to was known to be pretty wild – a happy, noisy place with a Minister whom the more staid clergy looked on with some suspicion. I told him I'd pop along next week.

But as the Sunday drew closer, I grew more apprehensive. I started getting butterflies. I wanted to chicken out. I had a vague inkling of what might be coming, and I was scared. I knew I was getting to the point where I was going to have to decide to do something. God was becoming real to me and the things I was reading and feeling were becoming over-powering. I began to realise there were fundamental contradictions in the way I was living and what I was discovering to be true. I just had this gut feeling that somehow going to this church on Sunday was significant. So I got to work.

I visited all my friends that afternoon, one after another, hoping one of them might suggest going to the woods for a joint, or a trip, or just getting drunk. Anything. But all of them were either out, or busy. That had never happened to me before. I realised all of a sudden that my excuses for not going to church were getting pretty thin. So I went to the student's union at Salisbury University and sat down at the bar with a beer, thinking to myself, 'Well, I'll just sit here and drink till I forget'. I drank fairly fast. It was really nagging at me, this service, and I was almost nervous.

After half an hour or so I looked up and to my relief saw an old acquaintance Barry Jobert, a real heavy hippie, walking towards me. He sat down and poured himself a beer.

'Hi Al.'

'Hi Barry.'

'Haven't seen you around?

I lent back and stretched my legs under the table. 'Oh, I've been around!' I remember looking at his face and smiling, I was so relieved to see him. 'What you doing here?

'As a matter of fact I'm just on my way to church. You know the Mabelreign Chapel? I just had a feeling tonight might be good.' He looked at my frozen face, 'Why don't you come?

I couldn't believe it. This guy didn't believe in God. He was a committed Hippie. This was too much. Here was I running out of excuses, retreating to the SU pub and somebody I haven't seen for ages walks in and tells me to go with him to the very church I knew I should be at. Someone was out to get me. So I said, 'No way, Barry, we'll be late. It's after six now. Lets go next week.'

He laughed, 'You don't have to worry about that Al.' Getting to his feet he swilled back the last of his pint. 'Come on bud, let's go.'

I had been taking drugs at a steady pace for six years and by this time I was pretty blase about hallucinations, but what happened during the next hour shocked even me. It was sunset as we drove through the town and when we arrived at the church there was a very happy person at the door to welcome us. That amazed me for a start. The most I'd ever got at other churches was a hymn book thrust in my face, but here was this person, not only happy himself, but for some reason happy because I was there as well.

We walked in and the place was packed. People seemed so relaxed, clapping their hands, singing, stomping their feet and doing all sorts of things. I was brought up Presbyterian and I was shocked! People do not enjoy themselves in church! I was quite staggered. I suppose I joined in the singing and things, I can't remember, but I do remember feeling that the Holy Spirit had come into the building and was there with us. And then I saw Jesus Christ.

He was standing in front of me and he looked just as I thought he should. I don't remember his face, I don't think I saw his face, but I saw his physical presence, the light, the warmth, the outstretched arms, and I knew that he was asking me to give my life to him.

Everything seemed to be happening at once, the whole room was pulsating, lights were flashing. It was a million times more spectacular than anything I'd ever experienced on drugs. It was as if the whole building was breathing. But these physical sensations were nothing compared to what was going on in my head.

When I actually saw Jesus I thought I'd had a heart attack. I remember feeling it knot up and stop. I thought it would never start again. I think it was panic. There was Jesus asking me to do something for him and the ramifications of that request were more than I could cope with. I couldn't understand it fully. All I knew was that what I was being asked to do would involve radical changes in my life. My security lay in the lifestyle and image I had built around myself; my friends, my drugs, the memories that were part of me. I felt Christ was asking me to leave it all, to leave the person that I thought I was, behind, and to take a step of faith into the unknown. And it was too much for me. I couldn't do it. I ran out of the back of the church, through the throng of worshippers, my mind reverberating with the one word, no no no no no no no no.

I found myself sitting on the steps outside and I knew what I had done. I knew I'd been face to face with the living God and rejected him. I thought, 'I've been given my chance and I've blown it. What point is there for living now? I looked up into the stars and quite honestly expected a bolt of lightening to sneak out of the sky and blot me out. I couldn't see any purpose in God allowing me to continue to exist. There I was, having rejected him to his face, what reason could there be for him to give a damn about me now. He could just wipe me out.

I felt empty, very empty. I don't think I felt remorse, just empty. And I began to pray for another chance.

I don't remember anything of the next two weeks except that I was praying. I don't even remember if I went to work. I was just praying for another chance. I was living under the assumption that I was about to be wiped out. Every situation I expected to be my last. I eyed every car with the thought that it was going to run me down. I may not have had any theology at that time, but there was no longer any confusion in my mind about who God was or who Jesus was. I just thought they would have no use for me anymore, that because I had rejected God, I was to be cast out of his presence for ever. Those two weeks really were a living hell.

But then one morning I woke up to a new feeling. I was totally at peace and I felt God was telling me that I was to have another chance. It was such a liberating and beautiful feeling that I was more than ready to say yes. I didn't have to think twice about it this time. I just got to my knees, 'Oh yes Lord', I prayed, 'take me home.'

Two weeks later 'Living Sound,' a Christian rock group, gave a concert at the chapel and there I publicly gave my life to Christ. I was put in touch with three excellent counsellors; a local minister called Gary Strong, who had arranged the concert, Terry Law, who was travelling with the group, and Don Norman, minister at the chapel. They took me through the scriptures, explaining what had happened to me and unwrapping the mysteries. Gary and Don were to remain close friends and counsellors for many years. In fact we still meet to share together the new challenges and demands of our faith.

But in those very early days I was still a freaked out hippie. All of a sudden a couple of things had happened to me that I couldn't deny; I'd found that God was real and I'd given my life to Jesus Christ. But that was as far as I understood. Apart from that my life was in many ways the same as it always had been. There was still a lot of unravelling to take place.

8. Finding Forgiveness

And yet it was not the same. There were some instant responses. For one thing I knew without doubt that I was a new person. The outward trappings of my life hadn't yet changed all that much, but inside I felt quite different. It was as if a thousand knots in my stomach had suddenly become untied. And I felt free, really free, from hate. Quite apart from the relationship with my family, which was healed and restored, I had a quite dramatic change of heart towards the police. It's hard, in the rational light of day, to express the sort of hatred I had for the cops. But at the time I was busted I really felt that I had been unjustly done in.

It was quite irrational, but in those days the police were Enemy No.1. We were the goodies, trying to live our own lives, not doing anybody any harm, and they were the gestapo, the heavy establishment, strong men harrassing us poor, peaceloving hippies.

The two guys who arrested me were on the top of my hate list. I used to dream about ways of doing them in, except that I wasn't by nature a very aggressive person, so it was more convenient for me to imagine them being run over by a bus or trampled to death by marauding elephants. But if I bumped into them on the street I'd start shaking. They were so much the enemy that to see them was a traumatic experience.

A few months after my conversion I did bump into one of them, Roy Welsh. He was in a garage having his car fixed and I'd pulled in for petrol. Before I knew what I was doing I had walked up to him.

'Hi Roy. Do you remember me?' I put out my hand.

Roy looked up from the wheel he had been examining, and being a good guy, shook my hand, but he looked a little surprised.

'Sure I remember you. Alec Smith. How are you?'

'I'm fine. I couldn't resist coming up to say hello.' I paused for a moment and he was clearly wondering what was coming next. 'I just wanted to tell you I've become a Christian. I've given my life to Christ. It's quite fantastic, man. You ought to try it!' 'That's great', he said, looking even more perplexed.

'Just wanted to tell you.'

It was only as I was driving away that I realised what I'd done and that I'd had no animosity in my heart for him at all.

On the contrary, I'd actually wanted to speak to him.

My feet had wings, though what poor Roy felt he was always too polite to tell me.

The other policeman had an even rougher time. His name was Dave Looker and he'd been the one who gave evidence against me in court. I felt God was actually asking me to go and see Dave, and to take him a bible. I used to bulk buy bibles in those first few months and practically stop people in the street to hand them out.

It was a strange feeling, walking voluntarily up the big wide steps of Salisbury Central Police Station and in through the dark doorway. I stepped up to the reception desk. The guy behind it was not smiling.

'I want to see Dave Looker, Drug Squad.'

'What's your name?'

'Alec Smith.'

'Is he expecting you?'

'No.'

The sergeant eyed me in silence for a moment, then he picked up a black phone, dialled two digits and waited for the ringing to stop. 'Dave? There's a guy down here called Alec Smith. He wants to see you. Will you send someone down?'

And then I waited till another sergeant appeared and led me in silence through the familiar corridor, past the room where my fingerprints and photograph had been taken and into Dave Looker's office. I had brought him a good hard backed version, and it was gripped pretty tightly in my hand.

I think Roy might have warned him, because he seemed less surprised and listened while I told him my news. Then I handed him the bible.

Funnily enough I met Dave in town only a few weeks ago. 'Hi Al', he yelled from his car window as he drove past, 'still got your bible.'

My relationship with my family improved from the first day. I started to understand my brother and sister as people, especially my brother whom I'd hardly known before. He was a bit older than me and we were so different. He lived in another world. We became real friends and it was as if family relationships just returned to normal – although they hadn't really been normal since we had been little kids on the farm all those years before.

Of course I tried to convert them all. For the first six months I was an absolute pain in the neck. I became an aggressive evangelist – but with no knowledge or wisdom, of course, just an overdose of faith. I bounced around so high on Jesus, I didn't need anything else. Most people didn't know whether to be delighted or sceptical, I think, and wondered whether this was just another way of freaking out. I remember my father did ask me one day if I ever did anything in moderation!

But I began to love and appreciate my parents again. As it happens it was a one-sided deal because I then realised that they had never stopped loving me. They didn't like me as a hippie and didn't know how to handle my involvement in that life-style, but they never stopped loving me, or trusting that everything would work out in the end. For the first time since we moved into the residence I can remember being happy at home, happy in their company and not feeling that I wanted to escape and be with my friends.

Dad never doubted my conversion. He was from the first delighted and very positive about it. He understood that it had to be extreme to begin with and that it would finally drop back and settle into a more balanced position – though he had no idea what it was to lead me into. Nor was there any doubt in my mind. Jesus had changed me from the bottom up. Before I had been a rebel without a cause, now my life had a purpose and vitality that it had never had before, and though I didn't yet know it, the Lord was preparing me to take part in a real revolution, and one that was to have a profound affect on my fellow countrymen, black and white, at a critical time in our country's history.

9. Black Anger

The only sympathy Arthur Kanodereka had ever felt for a white man was for a dead white man, and then only for a moment. Sometimes, when he looked down at the broken black and white bodies of the fighters in the bush with their stomachs shot out and their limbs distorted, then sometimes he had been forced to ask, 'Is this what God really wants? But it still didn't shake his fundamental conviction that nothing good could ever come from a white man and that open war was the only way left to secure freedom from oppression for his people.

When the guerilla war first started in Mount Darwin, in 1972, Arthur Kanodereka was the minister of the local black methodist church and his sympathies were entirely with the nationalist forces. He acted as a link man between the guerillas and the young Africans in the town, encouraging them to go into the bush and take up arms. He and his friends organised food for the fighting men, comforted them during the battles, gave them information about white targets and educated their hatred of the white regime.

It never occurred to Arthur for one moment that he had any obligations, as a Christian, to minister to the white population. His father had been a godly, warm-hearted evangelist who would talk about Christ to anyone who would listen, but not to Arthur. His training in the black college gave him a historical perspective of the white's intolerance and suppression of the blacks which fuelled his anger.

His sense of outrage and bitterness was heightened as he witnessed in daily life the insults and arrogance of the whites, their vanity and wealth, and the abject poverty and degradation of his own people. As he read the bible he felt it confirmed the righteousness of his anger. He came to feel he was licenced to hate and that his duty as a minister was to take up the nationalist cause.

And he suffered for it. Three times he was arrested by the security forces and three times he was tortured. He was electrocuted and strung upside down naked. By the time they cut him down he was almost frozen to death.

This reinforced the bitterness which seemed to envelope him. The only love he felt at all was for the young men he encouraged into the bush. These he tended and cared for as if they were his own sons.

Who could blame the Africans for feeling the way they did? My father's government was probably the most racist and repressive they'd ever been subjected to. Dad didn't see it that way, of course. He sincerely believed that the whites who had built the country out of nothing should be allowed to develop it for several generations longer. He was convinced it would take a long time before the black Africans were capable of running a modern, 'civilized' government. And there was no shaking him.

Not long after coming into power he sent Nkomo and other nationalists into restriction to a remote area of the country. They were followed by a steady stream of black leaders until all the most important were in detention or restriction. Then he outlawed their parties.

Perhaps it's worth pointing out that these nationalists were restricted without trial and in fact Dad's government increased the length of legal restriction without trial from one year to five, and they could always be re-detained after that.

When Dad got rid of the nationalists and banned their parties he closed down the last daily newspaper that was sympathetic to their cause. He would argue that he was trying to curtail the really awful violence that was prevalent at the time – with black fighting black – and he certainly succeeded, but he was also making quite sure that the legitimate arguments for black freedom were not going to be heard. To make sure there were no leakages he put the television and radio under government control. The leading newspapers remained more or less free, though even they had articles banned when the government felt they'd over-stepped the mark.

Unfortunately this government censorship didn't work both ways. If you looked through our national papers you could find published letters that expressed the most blatant racist views. The classic came from one right winger who even tried to argue that Jesus Christ himself had been white!

This public degradation of the black Africans was accompanied by a period of paranoia about Communism. Almost everything and everyone who disagreed with my father and his government were dubbed 'communist'. This wrote off quite a large portion of the world, especially after UDI when nobody much was on our side! All sorts of individual politicians, international financiers, the World Council of Churches and the American Peace Corps – to name but a few – were accused of having formed unholy alliances and one of Dad's MP's went so far as to call the United Nations 'the greatest communistic and devilish institution in the world'.

The Rhodesian Front's propaganda was that they were the only ones with the guts to build 'the real bastion for Christian civilization in Southern Africa.' But Dad's government was so blatantly anti-Christian that their insistence that they were upholding 'Christian civilized standards' against the onslought of socialism greatly harmed the cause of Christianity and made Communism seem infinitely attractive to the repressed and subjugated black.

But the ills of Africa began way back in the days of the early settlers. Right from the beginning the Africans objected to the way the whites had carved up the land for themselves restricting the Africans to Tribal Trust Lands which became over grazed and exhausted.

It sickened the Africans that a lot of white wealth was made from mining and agriculture – both industries absolutely dependent on cheap black labour. They flourished precisely because the low wages paid the Africans made them highly competitive on the world market. White labour would have been far more expensive. So the settlers grew rich and the indigenous population remained poor.

To put the record straight, there were always some whites who really cared about the Africans they'd settled among and who never supported the racist regimes. They built schools for them on their farms and looked after their health, but by and large the Europeans had no intention of sharing the wealth of this new country they'd found.

The other two areas of abuse that fired the nationalist cause were African health and education. Right up until Independence the health facilities for blacks were almost non-existant, while the whites boasted a health care as good as in Europe.

What alarmed the whites more than anything else – Dad included – was the prospect of an educated African population – that would really threaten the status quo. So the government's policy was to provide blacks with a technical education which would limit their employment possibilities almost exclusively to manual labour and to give them the absolute minimum of academic knowledge. With any luck, that would keep them in their place.

In a statement to Parliament in 1966 Dad's Minister of Education said he didn't think there was any purpose in education for the great majority of Africans, so long as they could read and write. The exceptions were teachers and nurses and a few low ranking jobs in the police force.

Many Africans would go so far as to say that Dad deliberately set about emasculating the African education system poor though it was, to make it even harder for Africans to get on. Certainly the population at that time was growing fast and Dad made cut-backs in the expansion of African education which meant fewer, in proportion, attended school. He also raised the school fees, which meant even fewer could afford to learn, and he detained many teachers for their 'nationalistic sympathies'.

I should make it clear that Dad was not one who hated black Africans. His relations with his workers on our farm for example, were very good. But his attitude was paternal, and he had no time for African nationalists with degrees who thought they could run the country better than the whites.

In the face of such determined and legalised repression, it was little wonder that men like Arthur Kanodereka felt the only way left to them was to take up arms.

10. Repentance and Commitment

All this had been going on without me realising it, but when I was converted it was as though the scales fell from my eyes. I began to see what was really happening in my country. I saw racial discrimination for the first time. I became aware of the daily degradation and humiliation of the blacks and the arrogant, unthinking attitudes of many whites – attitudes I had not thought arrogant before. I learnt, slowly and painfully, of my own insensitivity and began to see how my own selfish lifestyle had contributed to the bitter racial conflicts which were now erupting in a terrible civil war. At the time of my conversion the conflict between the black nationalists and my father's government were deepening. Many black and white Africans who had for years lived amiably side by side began to view one another with a new fear and suspicion. The blacks saw all whites as racists, as bigoted and corrupt, and the whites on their side began to feel that every black man must be a potential communist at least, if not a card carrying member.

By 1974 the war had been going on for a couple of years and I had been a Christian for 18 months, but I was struggling. I just couldn't go to church on Sunday, clap hands and say 'Praise the Lord' and not be aware on Monday that our country was being torn apart by a terrible war of hatred.

Surely there was an answer, a way through. I knew that my Christian experience was real and I knew that it had to apply to what was going on. There could surely be no problem too big for God to handle, no situation that was outside Christ's terms of reference. I was convinced that in a politically chaotic context, such as Rhodesia was then, God must have a plan.

Having been brought up in a political household and gone to a university where most of my friends were politically orientated, it struck me with new force that in the end it's the politicians who call the tune, who make the decisions. But Christians have had a real hang-up about getting involved in the political world. They're happy to convert a hippie here, or a business man there, but the politicians somehow exist in an area that is beyond Christ, on the other side of the abyss. For some reason we don't like to approach them, don't like to be involved, even though they may be taking our country down a very rocky road. I became convinced that since it's the politicians who wield the power, then it's among them that Christ's influence should be felt.

I came to feel that what was needed was a body of Christians who were prepared, under God, to work among our political leaders. But how? And what could I do? As I was turning this over in my mind, asking God what my part in all this should be, I met a most extraordinary group of people. They came from all sorts of different churches and from every walk of life. Some were students, some were civil servants. Some were university lecturers, some were housewives. Some were black, some were white. They had drawn together through the work of Moral Re-Armament, which at that time I had never heard of. The one thing they obviously had in common was the conviction that God, through the power of the Holy Spirit, could not only change the lives of men, but change the lives of nations. But we had to help him. We, as committed Christians, had to make our lives available to God so that he could use us for his work. But what exactly was his work? And how would he use us? Of one thing we felt sure – that a political solution alone could not solve Rhodesia's problems. Somehow there had to be a real healing between black and white, between tribe and tribe, if there was to be any lasting peace and we, under God's direction, had to help that healing come about.

In the December of '74 a group of us met in Bulawayo to decide what we should do. We believed absolutely that God had a plan for our country, if only we could put ourselves in a position to hear and understand it. As we studied and prayed together we came to feel that there was a need, not only for reconciliation between the different groupings in Rhodesia, but also between the individual and his family, the individual and God.

I shall never forget a remark Archie Mackenzie, a former British Ambassador to the United Nations, made to me once. He was talking about a typical UN meeting when fairly major international problems were being discussed. 'The problems on the table were immense', he said, 'But they were nothing compared to the problems sitting round the table.' He felt it was pointless talking about the divisions that separated America, say, from Russia, when the politician talking was estranged from his wife and children. A man had to be reconciled in his own personal life before he could begin to understand or implement reconciliation on a national level. We tend to look at politicians and believe that their being politicians has nothing to do with them being human beings. But I can't believe that your general emotional and moral health doesn't colour your political judgements.

As my friends and I talked and prayed about all this we felt God was urging us to organise an international conference that would air both sides of the reconciliation problem, the national and the personal. I felt very strongly that the aim of such a conference should be to bring about the change in people which alone would make political changes work. That meant including God.

I suppose in Europe an international conference of politicians and industrialists that took God into consideration would be regarded as pretty cranky. But not so in Africa. I think its true to say that God is much more real to Africa and the Africans than to England and the English. The traditional African is much more in tune with God than disorientated, sophisticated Western man. So while ours might have been regarded as a radical approach to a political problem, it was by no means regarded as a foolish one — as subsequent events were to show.

We felt the need to provide an unstressed atmosphere where delegates could get to know each other, man to man, without the tension of being quoted or reported. They then stood a better chance of discovering and discussing their common problems and their common ideals. There were, as far as we knew, no other opportunities for adversaries to meet in a non-confrontational situation.

We decided that our sessions should fall into two basic categories — the national, on subjects like Agriculture in Africa, Industry and Industrial Relations, and those on more personalised issues like bringing up children and family life. Some delegates would be invited to attend specific sessions only, others would be encouraged to spend the whole week. The date was fixed for June and we were each allotted our various tasks.

11. Hard Cash

As far as I was concerned the whole thing got off to a most inauspicious start. I teamed up with John Burrell, a young English guy my own age who'd just come back from Ethiopia, and we were 'volunteered' to arrange the accommodation. Eager to get going, we trundled up to the University administrator in Salisbury to book the premises and talk over the plans.

You'd have thought we were a couple of naughty schoolboys, the way the old man looked us over. He gave us twenty minutes of the 'I've-had-more-conferences-than-you've-had-hot-dinners' routine and pointed out that you needed considerably more than six months to organise an international conference with 400 residential delegates. A year at least. Not only that, but we could count ourselves lucky if half that number turned up. Quite apart from which it would cost us several thousand dollars and where did we think that sort of money was coming from in these troubled times.

This administrator was a very efficient guy, and it was quite true, he had run more conferences than we'd had hot dinners, but we felt that God had directed us to run this conference so, in some trepidation I must admit, we pitched our faith against his experience and went ahead. The university was booked.

That left the little problem of the running costs which we estimated at $30,000. Since John and I were also the finance committee it was up to us to find it.

Never will I forget those testing days. We literally walked the streets of Salisbury trying to raise the cash. The first man we went to see was one of the city's leading financiers who had a lot of sympathy for our work. When we told him what we planned, he laughed us out of court. Not a hope, he said. We'd be lucky to raise $5,000, let alone $30,000.

He was so adamant about the impossibility of it that he pulled right out, refusing to risk his name by being linked with a financial disaster. We had the same response from our other 'big gun', so there was nothing for it but to knock on all the little doors we could find.

We decided our best policy would be to tour the industrial area of town – that's about 25 square miles! Some firms we rang for an appointment, others we visited on spec. We had good days and we had bad days, but we tried to go into each interview with the idea of sharing our vision for reconciliation as much as for getting the money, and this helped to lessen the frustrations. And there was frustrations. But there were also singular moments when businessmen, despite their worldliness and the trappings of wealth, would catch a glimpse of new possibilities and their support – both moral and financial – spurred us on.

When the conference was over and it came to counting out the money we found our expenses had come to between $26,000 and $27,000. When I saw the first draft of the audited profit and loss account it showed a net profit of 48 cents. We had spent what we had raised. In fact more money came in afterwards that gave us profit we could use in later work, but that meeting of our needs reassured me that we were not mistaken, that God was working with us and that he would continue to work with us through all the impossible and painful days to come.

The other person who got a pleasant surprise was the University Administrator. In the event more than a thousand Rhodesians turned up for the sessions and we had our full quota of residential delegates. Among those who came were cabinet ministers and members of the opposing African National Council executive. There were African men and women just released from detention for their political views along with right-wing MPs. There were farmers and businessmen and national trade union leaders, black and white, and they were joined by delegates from 20 different countries. Clearly there was a willingness to see whether these Christians might not have an answer after all.

12. The Quiet Miracle

The opening session was attended by a galaxy of political big wigs. The Mayor of Salisbury said it was the most cosmopolitan assembly he had ever addressed, even before UDI. It was chaired by Sir Cyril Hatty, former Minister of Finance, and attended by the Deputy Prime Minister, John Wrathall. The ministers of Labour, Health and Finance were there along with the Deputy Minister in the PM's department. Sir Humphrey Gibbs, former Governor General was there and so was Pat Bashford, Leader of the Centre Party. Leading the African delegation was Bishop Muzorewa with members of the African National Council and there were many tribal chiefs from neighbouring countries.

In fact, looking back, it's not the content of the conference that I remember so much as the fact that such a gathering ever took place at all. We were a very isolated country cut off from the rest of the world by UN sanctions and by diplomatic, political and ecomonic boycotts. It's impossible to convey how out on a limb we felt, or how hungry we were for better communication. Yet despite the boycotts we'd managed to assemble a group of people from 20 different countries; representatives came from Britain, from the States, from the Scandanavian countries as well as from all over Africa. It helped us to put our problems, for once, into some international perspective.

For me the most significant participants were those from Kenya. Black Africa had a total boycott on communication with Rhodesia. It was amazing that they came, and the brightest hope of the whole conference.

As always at residential conferences much the most useful and challenging conversations took place over meals and at leisure times when people who would never normally have met could learn to relax together and relate as men and women, not just as antagonists. White MPs and black leaders who would not have been seen dead in one another's homes found themselves passing the salt and discussing mutual concerns. It was only the beginning of intimacy, but it was a beginning.

I think one of the things that threw many delegates off their guard was the honesty with which speakers discussed their relationship to God and to their fellow men.

Many of them, black and white, admitted to the problems of overcoming bitterness and racialism and their dependence on God to help them clear the junk out of their lives so they could start again. Some fairly eminent white men, including a South African High Court Judge, apologised publically for their past racist attitudes and admitted how much had been based on fear and ignorance. Many blacks witnessed to the power of God to help them put their hatred of whites aside. The remark that lives in my memory came from June Chabaku, a drama teacher from South Africa who said, 'If someone throws a brick at you, take that brick and build a home.'

This conference was an opportunity for myself too – as the much publicised renegade son of the black's most hated Prime Minister – to put my cards on the table. It takes quite a bit of courage, I can tell you, to stand in front of a large assembly and admit your wrong attitudes. Everyone knew I'd been a layabout and a junkie. Blacks and whites had an equal disregard and suspicion of me and who could blame them.

Before I began I leaned over to the man next to me on the platform. All through the previous speakers I had noticed a black clergyman looking like a thundercloud as he sat hunched at the back of the hall. He was a big man with a bushy beard and the sheer force of his antagonism was so great it seemed to radiate from him in waves. 'Henry', I said, 'who's that black guy at the back there – Do you know him?'

'Looks pretty aggressive doesn't he?', said Henry, screwing up his eyes to focus better. 'I think his name is Arthur Kanodereka'.

The consciousness of this man's obvious suspicion for the whole proceedings did nothing to increase my confidence as I rose to my feet. Briefly I told them what most of them already knew – about my past life and my newfound faith in Jesus Christ. 'Since then', I said, wondering if the words were going to come out in any sort of sensible order. 'I have come to realise that I had a personal responsibility for my country's dilemma. It was me, Alec Smith, who was answerable because my selfish lifestyle and insensitive attitudes had finally driven those boys into the bush.'

I thought it was too cheap to blame outsiders for our problems, like so many people were. It was fashionable then to accuse the communists of 'infiltration', or whipping up dissent among our normally 'happy young blacks'. But that wasn't true, and I felt I should say so.

'Those young blacks who leave their families, their homes, to trek 500 miles across the borders to join the guerillas are not happy', I said, 'nor are they communists. They're Rhodesians – abused, humiliated, frustrated Rhodesians. They might well be influenced by the Cubans or the Russians or the Chinese once they cross the border, but they remain Rhodesians, and its people like me who have sent them there. For my part, I am deeply sorry for the thoughtlessness of my past life and I have now committed myself to finding a solution for our country; to building bridges of reconciliation and to showing the rest of Africa that black and white can live together. That, under God, there is an answer.'

I sat down amid the clapping, my legs feeling a little shaky. Henry looked at me quickly and smiled.

My speech was followed by other pledges of support for a programme of reconciliation and of mutual accountability between black and white.

I was completely unaware of it at the time, but my confession that day was to trigger a most significant chain of events, the first of which took place in the heart of Arthur Kanodereka.

Arthur had only come to the conference because

his supervisors in the Methodist Church had insisted. He was extremely suspicious of the whole set up thinking we were out to brainwash black Africans, willing them into a false sense of trust in the white man's good intentions. He had learnt from bitter experience that white men were not to be trusted.

Yet, as I was speaking, something was happening to Arthur. Despite all his deeply felt hatred and suspicion, despite his knowledge of humiliation, his memory of torture, despite himself, he was profoundly moved by God's power to so obviously change the heart of man. He saw I truly was, in Christ, a new person; that I was no longer an enemy, but an ally.

'All I can say', he wrote later, 'was that suddenly my father's Christ became my Christ. I had a vision of what could happen. I saw Christ, the suffering Christ, not just for blacks, and not just for whites, but for all people. A care for white people that they should find something new came into my heart and I felt a new authority from God to give his message of reconciling love to all people, regardless of the colour of their skins. I realised that you could not change a man by hating him – you only made him worse – and I felt my hatred fall away.'

The shock of this revelation, this conversion really, was to profoundly affect Arthur. It was both painful and joyful. It was not only to transform his life, but to end it.

It was also the beginning of the most compelling friendship of my life. He opened the windows of my mind onto an Africa I had never seen or understood before. Through him I learnt of the very deep experiences of hurt the blacks had suffered at the hands of the whites. He exposed and revealed the depths of my own prejudices and above all it was Arthur who taught me to be truly colourblind. From that day until his death we worked closely and constantly together and neither of us had any doubt that only God himself could have brought together in friendship a black guerilla leader and the son of the white Prime Minister.

13. The Costly Friendship

His sudden change of heart meant for Arthur a reappraisal of many of his long held prejudices, personal as well as political. His hatred of whites had permeated his whole life. It had affected his relationships with his wife and his children; it had affected his praying and his preaching. It seemed to eat him up.

He also had to face the incredulity and suspicion of his friends. Here was a guy who had been brutally tortured by the whites and who, only a few months previously had been encouraging young blacks to join the guerilla forces – now he was sitting down in the white man's home and taking tea with him. Something had to be wrong.

But of course it wasn't Arthur's politics that had changed. He was still a passionate nationalist who believed and preached that there must be a quick transition to black government. It was just that he had come to see that violence was not God's way, that there was another, more powerful alternative to hatred. He came to realise that his opposition to white racialism had turned him into an equally rabid black racialist.

Our friendship began a few weeks after the conference when Arthur asked me to speak at his all-black church in the township of Harare. It was a startling suggestion. Harare was the Harlem of Salisbury, the centre of black consciousness. Thousands of blacks were crowded into poor tin houses and appalling hostel accommodation. Their dirty and overcrowded streets were only a stone's throw from the affluent white shopping areas where the jackerandas lined the street walks and the whites swanned around in shiny cars that their servants had washed and polished before breakfast. No white man in his senses would have driven through Harare township, let alone get out to go to church.

It was in the hostels that the most aggressive nationalists lived. These hostels had been built by the government to house single men who had come to the city to work. Because blacks were not allowed to own property in white towns or cities, or even live in a white area unless they were a white man's servant, there was no place for the black workers to live. They couldn't get digs, like they would have done in Europe. But the white economy was dependent on a high black labour force, which was cheap of course, so the whites built these huge hostels that looked like barracks and these were the only places available for the young Africans. They had no choice.

Living conditions were grim; only one lavatory to every 100 men; communal washing facilities and at least six to every small bedroom. Not surprisingly they became a hotbed of political activity. Many young men left them to join the guerillas in the bush, or harboured their friends when they came back into town. The hostels were also exactly opposite Arthur's church, on the other side of the road, and so his congregation was well sprinkled with some of the country's most bitter and hatefilled blacks. It was to them Arthur invited me to speak!

For some reason I agreed. I think I felt that Arthur must know what he was doing. I trusted him, but it didn't stop me worrying. The tension was particularly high at that time because 13 men from the hostels had just been shot dead in riots with the police so one way and another I wasn't too sure that they were in the mood to meet Arthur's new white 'friend'.

The whole evening was a bit like coming through an airline crash. I can't remember the details, but I can remember the event! I do recall that Hugh, a friend with long experience of Africa, came with me. Arthur had decided that we should show a film about William Nkomo, a great black South African leader who worked for reconciliation between the races. Then I should say a few words. Hugh and I were to arrive early to set up the projector.

Arthur's church was a simple building with a tin roof and a homemade stained glass window with a red cross. We arrived before everyone else and I remember placing the projector strategically level with the side door so that I could make a speedy escape in any emergency. I had visions of being trampled underfoot by teeming black multitudes!

The wooden benches were in place and the congregation just beginning to arrive when I realised I'd left one of the spools behind. I couldn't believe it! Hugh and I lept for our car and hared back through town – a good four miles – to fetch it. Hugh, an extremely experienced and sedate 'elder statesman', screamed round the corners and picked up a traffic violation ticket for crossing the red light. Finally we made it back to the church, not too late, only to find that it was crammed full of people and my carefully planned line of retreat had been blocked by three or four rows of big, black bodies.

Arthur led me to the platform out front and I remember wondering how I'd make it to the door if trouble broke out. The atmosphere was very tense. They'd only just buried their dead after the riots and I felt they wouldn't have been too averse to burying us, either. After all, we represented all that had insulted and humiliated them for generations and I, as Ian Smith's son, was an excellent target for revenge.

Arthur rose to his feet. 'Brothers and sisters', he said, and everyone stopped talking. 'I want to introduce you to the son of the man I hated most. Now I call him brother.' I could feel the mass of faces watching me. There was a force of concentrated antagonism, all directed at me, which set my hair on end. Arthur admitted later that he was quite scared himself. But not as scared as me, that's for sure.

As we showed Dr. Nkomo's film, the mood in the church gradually softened. It had several interviews with white South Africans who had come to see how wrong their previous attitudes had been. I don't think the congregation had ever heard a white man apologise before, and it took them by surprise.

But most important was Arthur himself. When Arthur changed, he started to change everyone around him. He wasn't one who could keep the truth to himself. He was extremely blunt and forthright, and when he told them about me, and the change of heart I had experienced, they believed him. If he said I was OK they were prepared, with reservations no doubt, to take his word for it.

It was extremely brave of Arthur. From now on he faced the threat of being listed as a 'sellout' – a man who had compromised on principles. You didn't do that when you were engaged in an armed struggle for your people's liberation. At least, you didn't do it and live. At every turn during the next few years he faced the possibility of being misunderstood and that, in those days, meant death. He was a man of authority, both within the nationalist party and among the black community, and they would rather have killed him than let him live a traitor to their cause. So it was quite a step for Arthur too, on that first Sunday, to stand up and commend to them the son of the white Prime Minister.

After the film I stood up to speak. I can't remember exactly what I said, but I think I told them about the way Christ had changed me and my commitment to the new Zimbabwe. I was so nervous that my brain went numb and I wasn't too sure what was coming out of my mouth. It got worse when I stumbled out the few sentences of Shona I'd been practising for days before.

The Africans are an extraordinary people. Time and again you will find in them a spirit of forgiveness that confounds the cynical West. This evening had been a traumatic and humbling one for me, and the congregation seemed to realise that. They accepted me on face value, they took me at my word. When it was all over they came up, every one of them, and shook hands with us all. Arthur started up a chorus and soon the church was filled with singing and dancing. That could only happen in Africa.

It was the first of many painful but important experiences that friendship with Arthur was to bring me. It's hard to put into words what it feels like for a black to tell you, with love in his heart, how much he hated you and all you stood for. You are completely defenceless before a man who can tell you of his hatred without hating. And it was Arthur who taught me by word and by experience, that reconciliation must start with the person abused.

That, I was coming to see, was the difference, the significance, of the Christian experience. It enabled you to tell someone the most painful truths, to be openly opposed to their most fundamental opinions, and to fight for them to be different, but to do so with love.

When I was a student the kids were trying to say something, but how did they do it? They spat at their lecturers, they vomited on desks. Do you think anyone understood what we were trying to say? With Arthur I was realising that naked hatred and aggression generate a fear in your opponent which only makes him more entrenched. Now we were beginning to learn that if you are truly seeking conversion in the heart and mind of the other man, then there has to be another way — but its a way that is more costly.

'Christ', wrote Martin Luther King, 'did not seek to overcome evil with evil. He overcame evil with good. Although crucified by hate, he responded with aggressive love.'

What contributed to my own motivation and total commitment to a new, integrated Zimbabwe, was the aggressive love of men like Arthur and other black friends who, continually committing their justifiable hatred to Jesus Christ, worked with charity and humour among the whites they moved among to bring about social change and reconciliation.

The first service, which we'd approached with such mixed feelings, started a new pattern of worship in Harare. Arthur had been wanting to create a nucleus of black and white working together and decided to try opening his church every Sunday evening for mixed worship, inviting people to come and pray together to discover God's way for our country.

I began to lead these services with Arthur. We were a sort of visual aid that black and white could not only live together, but actually work with each other and share the same ideals and goals for their society. This in itself was a startling revelation to many of the Africans there.

Arthur's one rule was 'no sermons'. He said we weren't there to be persuaded by men's rhetoric, but to listen to the spirit of God. He didn't want anyone to 'hijack' God's time! Nevertheless on the first Sunday he did speak, more than anything to explain to his congregation – for whom this was all a revolutionary idea – what his motives were. It says a lot for the strength of his conviction that he was able to persuade 300 men and women who had suffered so bitterly to open their doors to their avowed enemy.

The news of these 'mixed' services of prayer and worship soon spread round Salisbury and the church began to fill. Many eminent people joined us, as well as ordinary men and women who longed to find an answer to our civil distress. News also spread into the bush. Long after Independence former guerillas would come up to me and say; 'We couldn't say so at the time, but we were watching what you did and we were behind you.'

A year or so later after the first mixed service, when the war had heated up and President Wrathall called for a National Day of Prayer, Arthur's was the only African church to hold a service that day. He put an announcement on the front page of The Rhodesia Herald, our biggest newspaper, that all races were welcome. The church was packed out and there was even a member of Dad's Rhodesian Front party.

14. The Cabinet of Conscience

After that 1975 conference, right up until Independence, a nucleus of Christians began to meet regularly to pray and to seek answers to the current problems. This group became known as 'The Cabinet of Conscience', and to our gatherings would come a variety of other people, both black and white, Christians and non-Christian, who were also concerned to bring the civil war to an end.

Often that was all we had in common. Not all those who came shared the same faith as us, and certainly not the same politics, but we all cared for our country and were distressed at our people's sufferings.

Our meetings were always informal. There were usually about half a dozen of us and we'd spend a morning together discussing any current crisis and sharing ideas. We rarely prayed formally, because that would have embarrassed the non-Christians, but we did insist on a time of quiet after each discussion in which we could listen to God. It was during these periods of silence that ideas would come to us; people in government or power that we should be approaching, meetings we should hold, that sort of thing.

Any ideas that came would be discussed among all of us. Sometimes they were disregarded, mostly they were acted upon, and these we regarded as God's direction to us. From these quiet moments some significant actions sprang.

It wasn't always easy. If we felt God was asking us to befriend a politician we felt violently opposed to, that took some moral courage. We were also conscious that many of us were very ordinary people with no claim to fame, yet we were approaching some of the most influential, and sometimes the most dangerous, men in our country. But we were sure that we were called to be bridge builders, to bring enemies together to find a common ground.

The late Desmond Reader, who was a professor at the University of Rhodesia, was part of our Cabinet, and he felt God telling him one day to apologise to an African colleague whom he'd treated rather shabbily. Their subsequent friendship led to a series of meetings between right wing white politicians and African nationalists. Professor Reader and his wife gave informal meals in their home where the antagonists met, often for the first time. It took courage from everyone, but because the atmosphere was so relaxed and private, men who had previously held one another with scorn began to see in each other attributes they hadn't expected to find – intelligence, caring and a mutual longing to end the war.

But the war seemed a long way from ending. In fact it was steadily worsening. Casualities were increasing as civilians were being killed and injured.

Many were living under the strain of fear. The Africans were afraid of their own people who, having joined the raggle-taggle guerilla forces often launched attacks without rhyme or reason on fellow Africans. Whites, especially in the more isolated farm areas, were nervous of seige and viewed the future with increasing pessimism. Every month more than 1,000 whites were packing up and leaving the country for good. Dad put an electrified fence around his farmstead and took to wearing a gun.

15. Taking the Road

We could all see that the increasing violence would lead to a perpetuation of bitterness it would take generations to eradicate. We'd be avenging deaths for evermore. Although the 'revolution' we sought to bring about required repentance on one side, and forgiveness on the other – both such momentous steps that they could only take place through the grace of God – we also believed that we all had to recognise our mutual moral weakness; that to a greater or lesser extent we were all, regardless of colour, motivated by greed, or vengence or a desire to have power over another. I remember Arthur, when he was talking to some students about his own experience, saying; 'The colour of our skins may be different, but the colour of our sins is the same.'

In recent months we had seen that when people came together to explore the common ground of their humanity, miracles of acceptance and reconiliation took place and ordinary men and women, praying together, had found a common bond greater than their differences. No amount of fighting was going to solve the problem of how we learnt to live together, only learning to live together was going to do that.

After one of our 'Cabinet' meetings we felt compelled to push our work further afield. While the quiet meetings with political leaders continued in the capitol, we organised a mobile force of Christians from Africa and other parts of the world to tour some of the more strategic areas in the country where unrest was growing. Our aim was to bring black and white people together and to stimulate the sort of open conversations we'd held in Salisbury. We wanted to encourage people, to give them a glimpse of the new way we thought we had found and to excite them with the possibilities of a God-centred nation.

Arthur and I were still quite a draw. To most people, whatever their race, the thought of a black guerilla leader and the Prime Minister's son working and travelling together was mindbending. On both sides of the political divide they were wondering which one of us had sold out. We were regarded with the same sort of curiosity that met the bearded lady in a travelling circus. Nobody could quite believe that what they'd heard about us was true.

In June 1976, our 'Mobile force' hit the road. We

intended to use music and drama, as well as our own experiences, to get across the message of reconciliation we so passionately felt. But if we thought the world out there was just waiting to open its arms to us, we were wrong.

We started off in Que Que, one of the fastest growing industrial towns in the country, and our opening meeting had all the ingredients of a Molotov Cocktail. We'd been given the Globe and Phoenix Hall, and among the 300 or so audience was a posse of very vocal nationalist supporters who were, of course, all routing for Arthur. Mixed in with them was a Rhodesian Front MP, a handful of white farmers – all as tough as nails – and the Mayor of Que que who was aggressively right wing.*

Everything we stood for gave this guy a pain in his stomach. The thought that white men, like me, could possibly consider themselves to be, in any way, responsible for the civil war, or that men like Arthur could actually believe that majority rule was imminent, blew all his fuses. Instead of giving a vote of thanks at the end, he rose to his feet and bawled. Letters were sent to my father about what a bloody fool I'd made of myself and couldn't Dad do something about me, and the atmosphere in that hall was about as loving and forgiving as the Nuremburg Trials.

Bloody but unbowed we travelled the country addressing industrial groups, local organisations, school assemblies, churches – a whole range of public and private meetings.

The fact that we were committed Christians didn't impress the Africans one bit. Weren't the

*He eventually became an ally.

Rhodesian Front also Christians? What was it my father had said when he brought in UDI? That it was to preserve 'justice, civilization and Christianity'. The Rhodesian Front kept talking about these 'civilized Christian standards' by which they meant, of course, the maintenance of white supremacy and the acknowledgement that the African was an inferior being.

During their first years in office the newspapers were full of it;

'If the European is ousted from his pride of place, it could only be done by an intelligent race – a requirement that precludes the African.'[1]

'Every Christian who uses his eyes and brains knows without having to be told that Christianity itself could not survive without white supremacy.'[2]

Bishop Kenneth Skelton, when he was Bishop of Matabeleland, used to travel round the church schools only to be asked time and again by the African kids, 'Is it true what Mr. Smith says about Christian standards?' Because if it was, what self-respecting African would want anything to do with it.

So Christianity was a dirty word as far as many black nationalists were concerned. Even though many of them may have benefitted from missionary schools or hospitals, they found the Christian message utterly two-faced. They were taught by the ministers that all men were equal in the sight of God, but when it came to receiving communion, the whites went up first and the blacks second. Christianity was also inextricably linked with capitalism. As far as they could see all the ills of

[1] Liet. Col. Ichabod Allen in The Sunday Mail 19 August 1962.
[2] George Pile, Columist, Newsfront 3 April 1964.

Africa throughout the whole of colonial history appear to have stemmed from Western, capitalistic, Christian Europe.

To them, then and now, Christian capitalism equals oppression, equals colonization, equals exploitation and slavery and a raping of the country's resources. It's no wonder that Marxism, with its stress on liberation and a new social order, should be so profoundly appealing.

And the fact that the Rhodesian Front were so paranoid about Communism – to a really ludicrous degree – was an added conviction to the blacks that it must have something in it for them.

At one of our meetings in Que Que Christians were accused by a member of the ANC of 'choosing the sentimentality of Christianity without translating its ideals into action.' And that was right. The church was not then – and I believe is not now – anywhere near revolutionary enough. In fact it would be hard to imagine an institution less revolutionary or more staid and class conscious. But surely the gospel of Christ commands us to go out and work sacrificially for a more just and loving society. We're supposed to be an inspiration for the world. We should be leading the way. We should be moving faster and further ahead than any government thinking. The policy makers should be losing their breath trying to catch up with the body of Christ. It is we who should have been the first to voice the need for a new social order. What else can 'love thy neighbour as thyself' mean if it doesn't mean that you long for your neighbour to have all that you would wish to have yourself; good housing, good education, good health, good social opportunities and the freedom to make choices. How, as

Christians, can we bear to live in a society where others are so manifestly worse off than ourselves and whose dignity is so blatantly disregarded?'

Many people are against violence, but they've lost sight of the fact that it does violence to the human heart for people to live in poverty, want and degradation in the midst of plenty.

It's true that many of those we spoke to on our travels regarded themselves as Christians, and believed in Christ as their saviour, yet his teachings appeared to have had no practical effect on their lives. They did and thought things that were, by any stretch of the imagination, incompatible with Christ's teachings. There were those, for example, who saw no contradiction in being Christian and racist. Arthur, in the same way that he had not spared himself when he tried to dig out the roots of hatred and bias in his own soul, did not spare them.

'The church has been at work in Africa for some time' he said at one evening session, 'but people who have accepted Christ have lived as if Christ never lived, never died, never rose again. Preachers like me have preached a long time and never lived as Christ expected us to. This time we are calling people in Rhodesia, black and white, to dramatise Christ-like lives, day in, day out.'

16. Building Bridges

Arthur and I began to travel extensively together − not only in Africa, but in Europe. It was important for us both to see our country's problems from an international perspective. Rhodesia was so isolated from the rest of the world and we felt the need to break out of the cocoon. It was a bit like being in a maze when you can't see where you are but only the walls that hem you in. We were so oppressed with our problems that we couldn't see anything clearly. We also felt it important to tell the rest of the world what was going on inside the country, and to ask them for the sort of support we felt we needed.

While our visits to Europe were helpful to us personally, I suppose the most challenging trip we made was to South Africa. What an experience! For three weeks we were buffeted by prejudice and incredulity. In South Africa, of all places, the thought of the two of us travelling together crossed every rational concept of what was going on. We were viewed with extreme caution, especially by the black students who thought the whole relationship highly suspect.

I shall never forget the meeting we held at the coloured University of the Western Cape. We only gave them two hours notice, but even so five hundred students crammed into the hall, skipping lunch to attend. I think it was because they couldn't believe the billboard; 'Rev Arthur Kanodereka, Treasurer General of the African National Council and Alec Smith, son of the Rhodesian Prime Minister.' The mood was very strained. I was very strained! The students were highly motivated politically. Some had been imprisoned because of their opposition to the South African regime and it was official student policy that no contact with whites should ever be made. I didn't think they'd be throwing their hats in the air at the sight of me.

But I kicked off and we hammered home our message. And some of it rang bells.

They'd been very preoccupied that term with the horror Idi Amin was creating in Uganda, and although I probably didn't reach the real hard core, many of the students there could see that there had to be a change in the heart of man, as well as in the political system, if a just society was to emerge. While it was obviously too much for many of them to grasp in one short session that Arthur and I felt we really had found a new way, I think the straight talking and the obvious depth of our personal commitment to one another, as well as the mutual cause we fought, encouraged the sort of openness that was not too common.

It helped that Arthur was able to identify with their own feelings. 'I never thought that I could stand here beside the Prime Minister's son', he said, 'but he has changed, and I have changed.' He told them of his own hatred for the whites, his imprisonment and his bitterness as he saw his people suffer.

'But brothers and sisters, how can I tell you? I came to see it was my bitterness itself that was imprisoning me. With my bitterness gone, so was any spirit of submission or inferiority. Now I am a free man. I am a slave to no man, black or white. I am a free man.'

And Arthur looked a free man. After his death, when we used to sit and talk about him, recounting all he had taught us, all he had said, we often remarked how much Arthur had laughed. He was always laughing and his approach to every man and woman was always the same, regardless not only of their status, but of their views. He was open hearted to them and completely fearless in expounding the nationalist cause with a grace and humour that took the sting out of any potential antagonism.

Of course apartheid was in full swing during our

visit and restaurants and cafes refused to serve us both. He bore the perpetual insults with a buoyancy I found hard to emulate. But we had the last laugh when a friend in the South African parliament invited us to lunch in the members dining room.

Cape Town is the mother city of South Africa, the seat of parliament, the heart of apartheid. At that time there was a very small opposition party called the Progressive Reform Party – I think they had about twelve MPs – and among the right wingers there was a feeling that these men were really a breed of communist in disguise and ought to be banned. There was something, clearly, not quite right about them. This feeling was no doubt endorsed when the leader of the party invited Arthur and myself to see Parliament at work and to have lunch with him in the Members Dining Room.

It's hard to explain how sacred the hallowed precincts of Parliament are to the South Africans. Parliament is whiter than white. In the streets outside, and in the shops, black and white mingle as they go about their business, but not in Parliament. There you will not see a black face.

The waiters are white, the cooks and the cleaners are white, even the messengers are white. So when Arthur and I walked into the members dining room there was a moment of frozen silence when the other diners were immobilized through sheer surprise, fork loads of steak half-way to their open mouths.

When the initial shock had been absorbed and we were seated at our table you could practically see them thinking, 'Why doesn't someone put them behind a screen . . . or find them another room . . . or something', but this was clearly such an unforeseen predicament that there was no protocol to deal with it.

The most hilarious aspect of the whole episode was that Arthur, who had never been to South Africa before, was quite unaware of the stir his entrance had made. He laughed and chatted to the waiter as he asked about the soup and ordered his meal, oblivious of the fact that the poor guy was almost inarticulate with shock. We all enjoyed the meal immensely.

We saw a lot of people quietly during our stay; journalists of all persuasions, white politicians and senior black leaders. Even the 'Die Transvaler', traditionally the voice of conservative Afrikanerdom – and you can't get more died in the wool than that – had a mug shot of us captioned 'Historic Visit'. Our friendship was referred to as 'a miracle', and so it was. Everywhere we went, just by being together, we witnessed to Christ's power to change lives, and through changed lives, we hoped, to change the course of history.

17. Father and Son

There's no doubt that during these years my father's attitudes softened. He'd probably never admit to it, he's a politician and politicians don't readily admit to things like mistakes or a change of heart. But over a period of four years or so I exposed him to men who had a different way of looking at things. I was to introduce him to people he would never normally have met.

Most Prime Ministers are very isolated from the real world, and Dad was no exception. He would meet those whom his advisers thought he should meet, or men who he wanted to meet – predominantly right wing politicians. In Europe, for example, he'd home in on Franz Joseph Strauss from Germany, or Jesse Helmes from the USA. They'd be people who would shake his hand and say, 'You're doing a good thing, old boy, keep it up.' It's a trap most politicians seem to fall into. They feel a bit uncomfortable with people who criticise them. It's much less fraught to be with your own kind who pat you on the back.

But I did introduce him to people – in the privacy and quiet of our home – who had different points of view. They didn't come to argue with him. There would have been no point in me wheeling in the opposition and sharpening the sabres. He could get all the opposition he wanted in the political arena. No, these men, by and large all committed Christians, were people who were deeply concerned for him as a person. They brought love to him as well as a different opinion.

When Dad met Arthur it was the first time he had ever met a black nationalist socially. He'd met them across a conference table where they'd come in from prepared positions, talked across the table and left – rather like two boxers walking into an arena from their respective dressing rooms, fighting and walking back to their corners. But he'd never had a real conversation with a nationalist. Nor had a black African ever set foot in our home for a purely social event. Dad's only experience of them was in a political confrontation or in the master/servant relationship.

When Arthur and his wife Gladys came to tea,

that was a revolution in itself. (Especially for my mother who is a true blue South African!) But the two men just sat and talked. They didn't get embroiled in any great political arguments. Arthur didn't make any dramatic accusations or demands. He just wanted to get to know who this Ian Smith was. There was no longer a trace of hatred in him and Dad was bowled over by his sincerity and his courage.

The guerillas were an absolute anathema to Dad. He used to refer publicly to Mugabe as 'an apostle of Satan'. He had no sympathy or understanding for their methods or their point of view. Yet despite that, sincerity and courage are the two qualities he places above all others in his fellow man, and in Arthur he found them both.

When they had gone we sat on the verandah together, another pot of tea brewing quietly on the wicker table and the dogs lolling in the heat.

'Alec, I really want to thank you for bringing Arthur and Gladys here. If all black nationalists were like him, I'd have no trouble handing over the country tomorrow.'

For Dad to conceive that a black African nationalist could actually run the country was some break through! I remember sitting in silence, unable to think of anything to say.

They met several times after that and what got to Dad was the frank way Arthur could admit his past hatred and his determination now to avoid all bitterness. Seeing other people's point of view is not always Dad's strong point, but he is nevertheless, an astute judge of integrity, and he admired Arthur for his.

During these years my own relationship with him grew stronger and stronger. Of course he thought I was fairly crazy. I know I used to exasperate him at times because he couldn't really understand why I didn't agree with him! Although he admires what he calls 'idealists', he did feel that my friends and I had got our feet too far off the ground. We didn't face up to the 'facts' of life as he would have liked us to. Not pragmatic enough. What he meant, of course, was we didn't see things his way! Yet our disagreements were always friendly, always conducted in an atmosphere of family love which I had come to value very much.

Dad would call himself a 'God-fearing man'. He feels he has strong principles based on God's laws, which were part of his background and upbringing, so while he was certainly sympathetic to our commitment to Jesus Christ, he did think we took it all just a little too far.

'You know Alec', he said during one of our evening chats, 'I think you're inclined to put a little too much faith in God. Now, don't get me wrong son. You know I'm a believer, but you can't put your faith completely into your religion and believe that it's going to deliver all the good for you. I've found in life that that just doesn't work.'

Well, I might not have been able to convert him to the power of Christ, but there was an important change going on in his perceptions, whether the old man admits it or not. I am convinced that his conversations and liking for Arthur helped him to understand Mugabe when they met secretly just after the 1980 elections. It was a meeting with profound significance to the country since it undoubtedly helped to avert the threatened military coup which would have plunged our country into another long and bloody war. The two men at that time found an unexpected respect for one another which I'm sure would not have been possible had Dad not been quietly exposed to some remarkable black men and women in the years before.

In fact Dad surprised the world when, in late 1976, he went on television to announce to the nation that he had accepted the principle of black majority rule. That was a long time before the Lancaster House talks and we had some bloody years to live through before peace came, but it was the first step. He had come from a position of saying 'Never in my lifetime. Never in a thousand years', to saying 'In the foreseeable future.' It was a big leap. He told me later that when he had been sitting in front of the camera making that statement he had felt God's hand on his shoulder.

So during these first years with Arthur we were all, in one sense, quite excited because our work seemed to be gathering momentum. We had the ear of a number of influential men and the grass roots enthusiasm seemed to be growing. And yet it was just a drop in the ocean. It was like trying to run up the down escalator. The overall situation was getting dramatically worse. Diplomatic solutions were dying on their feet as one conference after another bit the dust – the Victoria Falls conference in 1975; the Geneva Talks in '76; the Anglo-American proposals of '77 – all ended up a cul-de-sac.

Meanwhile the average death toll had risen from eight to thirty a day with many more injured and homeless. Stories were percolating through of terrible atrocities – perpetrated by both sides. There was an increasing fear that the situation would run away with us. Civilians were being caught in crossfire between the Security forces and the guerillas. Sometimes there'd be a shootout between opposing guerilla forces. It was developing into a chaotic free for all. The guerillas would descend on African villages to rape, loot and murder, demanding hostages and forcing the villagers to give them food. Next day the white security forces would seize and torture the villagers for information. It was horror upon horror.

18. Elisabeth

Elisabeth was different. I met her only a few months after I first met Arthur. I'd gone to Switzerland to a Conference for young people at a place called Caux above the lake of Geneva where there is an international centre for Moral Re-Armament. There were about 100 of us helping and we'd been split into smaller working groups of about 30 and given specific tasks. Our group was responsible for meals. We had to plan the food, sometimes help to prepare it; we had to lay the tables, serve at meal times and organise the buffets. We also met in the mornings as a discussion group, sometimes to pray and study the bible, sometimes to talk about social and political problems.

Right from the start Elisabeth stood out from all the rest, not just because she was beautiful, which she was, but because of her wonderfully peaceful vibes. It's hard to put into words, but I just liked what I felt her to be. As I listened to her joining in the conversations I found I was in harmony with her somehow. There was something about this lady that gave me a sense of peace and belonging.

And that's how it was. No fireworks, no blinding flashes of light. We had no deep tete-a-tetes – in fact I don't think we talked alone much at all. I just watched her and listened to her and gradually the conviction grew that this was someone special.

Then the crowd of youngsters decended on us – several hundred of them – with their walking boots and their transistors and their expectations and problems and demands.

They came from all over Europe and among them, I must say, were some very pretty girls. Yet still, through the ensuing weeks of hubub, Elisabeth wove her way in and out of my days. And then, one morning, she was gone.

The youth conference had finished and most of the crowd had gone home leaving the working parties to plan for the next session. I had assumed that Elisabeth was, like most of us, there for the season. But this particular morning she didn't turn up for the meeting.

I kept looking for her all through the day, expecting her to walk into a room, or down the stairs. But she never came. By late afternoon I was getting really restless. I walked down to the Post Office for my mail and looking into her box, found there was a letter for her. That was comforting. She must be coming back soon. Perhaps she'd just gone off for the day? I'll take this letter back for Miss . . . ' I said to the Post Mistress, trying to sound nonchalant.

'No, don't worry', she hardly looked up from her work, 'She's gone back to Norway. I'll send it on to her there.'

Gone back to Norway? Gone back? I couldn't believe it. I felt quite indignant. How could she go back? In my mind I had visualised the rest of the summer stretching endlessly before us. I had just assumed that our relationship would unfurl in a sort of dreamy, continuous delight. How could this girl just up and leave in the middle of it? I felt almost angry.

That night I wrote a long letter – for me a sure sign of disturbance since I normally can't even manage a postcard – and poured out all my confused and turbulent feelings for her. Without delay she replied. Her letter was blunt and to the point. She told me in terms that left absolutely no room for doubt that she felt nothing for me whatsoever.

I was flattened, destroyed. The whole sandcastle in my mind had been crushed by a tidal wave. I don't think I've ever come down to earth with such a thud before. It was like falling out of a ten storey window. Her letter had left me without the faintest glimmer of hope – it had been like putting out a match with a fire engine.

Like a man concussed I made my way to the railway station and took the next train to Geneva. I arrived at 9.30 in the morning and walked into the first pub I found. It didn't even occur to me to pray. I had no thought at all about God, my only concern was to obliterate the pain. I tried every kind of pub and every kind of beer the town could offer. I saw Geneva from every angle, including the gutter. I was stoned out of my tree for a day and a night.

I eventually woke up in the railway station sleeping on a bench with a crowd of other drunks and hippies. In the cold light of morning, with a terrible hangover and a loose stomach and no money in my pocket, I was full of remorse. I felt very guilty, very sad. Fortunately I had a return ticket in my pocket and so I crawled my way to the train.

I couldn't face going back to the Conference

centre, not straight away, so I rang up John McCauley who was now working with the L'Abri foundation in the next valley. John and I went back a long way together and had enjoyed some narrow escapes in our druggy days – though he'd never been as wild as me. Now he too was in full time Christian work and I knew that I could trust him with this terrible pain and remorse that I felt.

He was a good friend. We walked, we ate pizza at a little Italian restaurant, we drank coffee and we prayed. I was able to pour out the whole story of Elisabeth and the way I felt. I remember he talked to me of God and helped me to get things into some sort of perspective, but mostly he just listened, and I was so grateful to him for that.

And in a sense, that was it. The whole two days experience had been so intense it seemed to anaesthetize the pain and with my mind, at least, I understood that it was over. The situation was so hopeless that I just blotted her out. The summer passed and my life went on.

Two years went by in which a couple of girls came fleetingly to my notice, but not in any desperate sense. I was pretty wrapped up in my work, which was absorbing, and my emotions had quite enough to cope with what with the war and my trips with Arthur.

In the summer of 1977 I was invited to London, around the time of the Queen's silver jubilee, primarily to appear on a TV programme. On the spur of the moment I decided to travel back to Rhodesia via Switzerland and call in at the Centre just to see what was going on and if I could lend a hand for a few days. It didn't even cross my mind that Elisabeth would be there. I had long since ceased to think of her.

But she was there. As soon as I walked into the dining room I saw here and the whole dark episode came flooding back. I stood still for a moment by the door, stopped in my tracks, and she must have sensed me. She looked up and I saw that she too, was troubled.

We were put in the same discussion group, quite by accident, and whenever we established eye contact across the room I could sense that a lot more was going on than just a nodding hello. It was like talking to somebody with words and thinking something else at the same time. I could see she was having as much trouble as me, but I didn't know quite why. My feelings veered from thinking one moment that she was just disturbed because this clown from Africa had come back to embarrass her, to wondering if, perhaps, she did feel something for me after all.

That night I prayed and it came to me very clearly that we just had to sort it out. We had to get away somewhere and talk it through. It was four days before I could bring myself to ask her, and the next morning I was flying home.

We had arranged to meet in the Library, but there were too many people about so we walked slowly down to the railway station and ended up at the cafe where we ordered some of their fearful coffee. And we talked.

Elisabeth told me all about herself. When we had first met she had been very much in love with someone else. He was a young minister, very committed, who wanted her to marry him. Humanly speaking it seemed an ideal match. Elisabeth told me she really longed to accept, but as she was praying about it she felt convinced that God was asking her to say no. It hadn't been easy.

I could understand that and I was so glad she had told me.

After that we spoke mostly about Africa. I told her about our hopes for a peaceful settlement and the work we'd been doing behind the scenes. I told her about Arthur and my Dad and the way the war was going.

By the end of the evening our coffee had grown cold and my eyes had hardly left her face. But we both felt so free, relieved that we could look at each other straight and not hide our feelings. We had a great sense of friendship and security. As for me, it became clear to us both that I was as hopelessly in love with her as ever. She was understandably wary of responses from the heart, but even so I heard her say words I had not allowed myself to hope for, that she was falling in love with me.

That night, unknown to each other, we both prayed; we both committed our total lives into God's hands, each of us relinquishing responsibility for our future to him. When we parted the next day we had made no plans of our own. We decided we should make no contact with each other at all. If God wanted us to marry he would bring it about; if he didn't, then we would rest happy with his decision. We had given him the steering wheel and it was an incredibly liberating experience.

I went back to Africa and got stuck into my work, quite convinced that God would tell me what to do about Elisabeth when he was ready. And that's exactly how it worked out.

About a year later I was sitting in the army canteen during a call-up. We were all very depressed indeed about the war and I was feeling pretty low. The other guys were talking about their wives and families and I suddenly thought, 'This is it. I'm to go to Elisabeth.' I had no doubts about it at all, the only trouble being that I had no idea where she was. I didn't know what she was doing and I didn't know who she was with. I had had no news of her at all. For all I knew she could have been married to someone else. So while I had this clear feeling that God was telling me to go to Elisabeth, I had no idea where she was, what she was or even who she was.

As soon as I could leave I went into town and bought an airline ticket for Europe. I remember thinking it was a heck of a lot of money to shell out on just a 'feeling'. Anyway, I decided to go to the Conference Centre because that's where we'd always met and I assumed that's where she'd be again.

Three weeks later I was on the plane to Switzerland, fully expecting to stroll in and find her ready and waiting. But I was wrong. When I eventually arrived she wasn't there.

For two weeks I waited, scanning every new face that walked into reception, hanging around the hall for every coach load of arrivals. She never came. I couldn't believe it. Was God playing some sort of joke on me?

In the end, in some desperation, I spoke to the one man I knew Elisabeth was close to, Jens. Against all my instincts I told him the whole story. He listened very patiently, not letting on by so much as a twitch of his eyebrow that actually he'd heard it all from Elisabeth a year before. When I eventually stopped talking he advised me to write to her telling her how I felt. He didn't think it fair to spring a proposal on her unannounced.

But I couldn't write. Letters have never been my strong point, and in any case I felt too uptight about the whole thing by then. I'd been convinced that God had told me to come to Europe. I'd spent a small fortune on the airfare and somehow just sending a letter seemed all wrong. And I was fed up. I remember muttering at God, 'OK, OK, I've had a nice time. It's been great fun and now I'm going back to Africa', and with a mental pout I slammed the door on the future and turned my face for home.

You have to go to Africa from Switzerland via London, so I rolled up to Geneva airport ready to catch the next plane. I wouldn't have to wait long since there are usually eight or nine planes a day to London. As it happened I missed the first plane and all the others were booked. Nothing more till the morning.

What a drag. I rang up a friend and arranged to spend the night, left my bags at the airport and began to mooch around Geneva, my memories returning inevitably to that other day, three years before, when I'd also had time and thoughts to kill.

As I was having my third cup of coffee I got it into my head to phone her, just as a last chance, a parting shot. I don't think I had much hope of finding her in and I hadn't worked out at all what I'd say to her if I did.

Finding a quiet booth I dialled her number. Phoning long distance in Europe is quite eery. You just pick up the phone, dial the number, and the next thing you know, you're ringing in Norway, or Sweden or Iceland. The trouble is you don't know what you're ringing. All the sounds are different and I was convinced I'd got an engaged tone when a woman's voice said in Norwegian something I presumed to be 'Hello'.

'Hello', I said, feeling a bit silly, 'Please may I speak to Elisabeth?'

'Yes, this is Elisabeth speaking, Alec. I was expecting your call.'

I spent three days in Oslo with Elisabeth's family, waiting. She had had a dream the day I rang that I would be in touch with her, but the dream had not told her what to reply! For three long days we talked and walked. I would have gone plop into marriage without a second's hesitation, but Elisabeth wanted to make quite sure that God had given us his blessing. I used to return to her cousins at night and they'd feed me tea and cornflakes before I went to bed and watch discreetly at a distance while my hopes once again flickered and died.

I think God often brings you to a point of surrender before he gives you what you long for. It partly proves to yourself that your obedience is greater than your desire. That's how it was with me. On the fourth morning, as I said my prayers, I relinquished Elisabeth once and for all to God. I came to a place where I could accept 'No' as an answer. I knew that my love for God and my desire to serve him was greater than my longing for Elisabeth, but the knowledge did not bring me any joy. I longed to marry Elisabeth. I loved her and I wanted her, but I finally let her go.

That morning she was to visit me, and as I heard her walk through the front door I braced myself to tell her the decision I had come to. She walked in looking so lovely.

'I've got something to tell you', I said, wanting to get it over with. 'Yes', she said, 'and I've got something to tell you'. Something must have made me pause in my rush to speak.

'You start', I said.

'I'm sure of the answer now Alec. It's yes.'

It still surprises me that two people who were so different in upbringing and who knew so little about each other could have felt so much as one. Yet our lives have fitted together like a jigsaw puzzle and the picture makes sense.

If I had contemplated marriage before Elisabeth it would have been to someone from my own country – from Britain at the very outside – to someone whose roots I could relate to. But a Norwegian! Yet we have an understanding of each other I still find amazing.

The whole business of waiting and trusting God was very important for us. We feel our marriage to be rooted in his will. We know where we came from and we know where we're going to. For Elisabeth and I there are no back doors, no escapes from one another. When the difficulties come – which they do in most marriages – then we have the confidence of knowing that God will teach us and guide us through.

Elisabeth and I were married in Oslo on 9th June, 1979. After a few weeks honeymoon amid the fjords and the forests and a host of family and friends, she packed her few belongings and brought her life to Africa, and into mine.

19. Bitter Conflicts of War

War changes everyone. I had to do my army call-ups like every other young white. For whites in general it was a fairly terrible time. We spent six weeks on call-up and six weeks at home. This went on for years and with devastating effect on the home and working life of many families. Some young Rhodesians who had their studies interrupted like this for year after year never finally achieved their training. Marriages were put under constant strain as women learnt to cope, often in very hard situations, without their men, and then had to make the constant emotional readjustments when they returned. There was also the tension of fear that we all lived in and which permeated our homes and our personal relationships.

For myself, working as I was with black nationalists whom I loved and respected, fighting was a peculiar nightmare. Consciencious objectors were not recognised, so if I'd refused to fight I would have been imprisoned and immobilized and the work that Arthur and I could do together put to an end.

Besides which at first, when the war began, before I knew Arthur, I had believed the propaganda the government was putting on. They painted a picture of the nationalist forces as pure Marxist. And indeed, Mugabe himself made quite clear his allegience to the Marxist ideology. Because most of us only met guerillas at the end of the rifle, how were we to know any different? So as a Christian I believed that I had a just fight on my hands.

It was only as I learned more from Arthur that I began to see through all that. A 'Marxist terrorist' is everyone's idea of the person you're allowed to hate. We were encouraged to feel no remorse at the thought that we'd killed such a one. But when you realise that in fact the person you have killed is a nationalist, a fellow Rhodesian, a fellow citizen, who out of sheer frustration and a lack of any other alternative has taken to force as a way of expressing his anger and righting the wrongs – then that totally changes your perspectives.

The more I learnt from Arthur the more painful it

became. The truth was that for the main, the guerilla army was composed of black Africans who were primarily concerned with freedom. Of course there were Marxists among them, but by and large it was a nationalist war and they were fighting for their freedom and dignity, not for Marxism.

Those who have never fought a war really don't understand what it's like to know that there are a bunch of strangers lurking behind the hill waiting to kill you. Armed to the teeth with all the latest sophisticated firearms and hand grenades, there is no way they are going to stop and ask your political opinions before pulling out the pin. It's not a situation where you sit down and philosophize, weighing up the pros and cons of pacifism. Once in combat it becomes a question of 'them and us'. They become 'the enemy'. Your primal instinct is to stay alive and you become as cunning as any other hunter and hunted. That was what was so morally and emotionally disorientating about the whole war game.

Then I'd come home and meet with some of the guerillas and their supporters in Arthur's church. We'd talk our problems over together. We all felt the same, as if reality was suspended and we were playing some terrible game that had somehow got hold of us. Many of them, too, while believing in the cause, hated the violence, but would have been branded traitors and probably killed had they left the fighting. We were all trapped and confused by our own propaganda.

Arthur used to pray with us before we went back into the bush — not that God would help either side to win, but just that he would protect us. That's all we could do — pray for one another. Then we'd take up our guns and play out this macabre and heartbreaking charade. The truth about war is that everyone loses.

As it progressed, and my understanding changed and grew, so also did the internal conflicts I experienced. Unravelling propaganda and the false emotions that combat engenders in you is a long and painful process. Yet the more I had to fight the people I wanted to be reconciled with, the more determined I was to try and bring understanding between our two sides. I took every opportunity to preach reconciliation and to open up with the men I was with the new perspectives Arthur had taught me. Most of those men, many of whom had been in the army for years, had never really heard the story from the other point of view. As the war progressed they were increasingly willing to listen, and of course they had read about my work with Arthur in the press. They also realised that it wasn't easy. They'd been with me when my friends had been shot, when they'd fallen at my feet with their stomachs blown out. They knew that talk of reconciliation was not glib.

There were some aspects of the war I could never accept, and never forget. I remember an incident when we were ordered to shoot a two year old boy. He was running where he shouldn't have been, too frightened to listen to us calling. My colleagues raised their rifles and shot. I didn't, I couldn't, and I would have been very happy to explain my reasons to the court marshall.

Meanwhile world pressure was growing for Dad to settle with the ANC. Our neighbours, especially, Zambia, Tanzania and Mozambique, were becoming increasingly involved as guerilla activities spread over their borders. Everyone was afraid this would escalate into a full scale African bloodbath with East and West staking their claim for a piece of the cake. (Quite apart from British and American interests, Nkomo's forces in Zambia were being armed and financed by the Russians and later Cuba, and Mugabe's forces in Mozambique were getting help from the Chinese). Martial law was in operation over most of Rhodesia and the guerilla tactics were becoming more sophisticated and devastating in their results.

Mugabe and Nkomo were beginning to get their act together and had formed a rather loose liaison called The Patriotic Front. It was a fairly suspicious friendship because of the ideological and personality differences between them. Mugabe didn't like the fact that Nkomo was so dependent on Russia and Mugabe himself was ideologically much more highly tuned. Most people felt, I think, that Nkomo was a man with a price. But whether you agreed with him or not, it was clear that Mugabe could not be bought. At the time Nkomo's men were better trained as soldiers, but Mugabe's men were better infiltrators. They held meetings at night in the villages explaining what they were doing and indoctrinating the people. Between them they made quite a formidable force.

Against this background of consolidating opposition my father and Bishop Muzorewa finally came to an agreement and drew up the details of a transitional government which was to lead to independence under black rule on 31st December, 1978.

An interim government, known as the Executive Council, was to be set up with Dad handing over the reins to Bishop Muzorewa. Parliament was to stay more or less as it was except that the nine ministerial posts, instead of being held by one man alone, would now be held by two, one black and one white, in joint ministerial positions. The supreme war council, however, was to stay firmly in white hands, at least until the expected General Elections the following Christmas. Dad, looking less than jolly, signed the agreement with Muzorewa in Salisbury on March 3rd.

20. The White Man's Puppet

Our jubilation was tinged with hesitation. We had come to see ourselves as a yo-yo society — bouncing up and down between expectation and despair. So many hopeful schemes had, in the past, ended in nothing: the talks on Fearless; talks on Tiger; the Alec Douglas-Home agreement. Yet there were those of us who did feel that this time the end of white minority rule really was in sight. And for some of us — Arthur and myself included — it was a time of short lived euphoria. Even the blacks we spoke to were quietly hopeful. From a historical point of view they had every reason to be suspicious because none of the plans so far put up by the whites had ever had anything in them for them, but Arthur, who by this time was Treasurer of the ANC, was also appointed chairman of the committee for contact with the guerillas. He went repeatedly to see the boys in the bush, often risking his life, to encourage them to accept this March 3rd agreement. And many of them did and were ready to lay down their arms, hopeful now that what they were fighting for had finally been achieved.

Outside the country the 'March 3rd Agreement' was greeted with far less enthusiasm. The Patriotic Front, who had not been consulted in any way, saw it as a cop out. The rest of the world saw it as a cop out. The British and the Americans rejected it. The UN Security Council rejected it. The Organisation of African Unity rejected it and our neighbouring states rejected it. And within a matter of weeks we too were forced to face reality.

I think we were partly fooled because the initial moves of the new government, apparently under Bishop Muzorewa's leadership, did seem so positive. On an everyday level many of the colour barriers were broken down. You could no longer refuse to serve people because they were black; hotels were open to all citizens and more African kids were admitted to white schools. On a national level the ban on operations of Nkomo and Mugabe's parties (ZANA and ZAPU) were revoked; political detainees were released; the government promised to dissolve the 'protected villages', which were a sort of house arrest for villagers thought to be vulnerable to the guerillas; an amnesty was offered to any fighter who wanted to come back home.

It soon became clear that things were not as good as they seemed. New legislation was passed that was supposed to abolish discrimination in the areas of land tenure, housing, education and medical facilities. What actually happened was that privilege by virtue of colour was replaced by privilege by virtue of wealth. You no longer had to be white to have it all, just well off — which in Africa, of course, meant exactly the same thing.

It also became clear that there wasn't going to be

any serious attempt to hand over power.

Africans were not being promoted to senior positions in the country and the army and airforce were still in the hands of the whites. For us the real crunch came when Byron Hove was sacked as co-minister of Justice, Law and Order after only one month in office.

Byron Hove was a close friend of Arthur's and would sometimes join our 'Cabinet of Concience'. He was a very gifted young lawyer and we were so delighted when he became a co-minister. He'd only been in office a few weeks when he made what was quite a mild speech, in the circumstances, suggesting that there should be a more rapid promotion of Africans in the legal service and police. Until that time no African could be promoted higher than Sergeant, even if he'd been in the Police Force for 30 years, and there were very few blacks in senior positions in the judiciary.

His suggestion brought down a thunderbolt of Caucasian wrath. The whites were horrified. The police and judiciary were hallowed sanctities of white supremacy and the thought of blacks being promoted was sacrilege to them. Dad told Muzorewa that this new minister, Byron Hove, would have to go, and Muzorewa told Byron Hove. With that event our whole faith in Bishop Muzorewa as a leader for black Africa crashed to the ground.

Arthur reported that contact with the guerillas dried up immediately. It was clear to them, and to most other blacks, that the whites still called the shots. They accused the Bishop of being a mere puppet with the Rhodesian Front pulling the strings.

It was a sad and bitter time. Muzorewa was without doubt the most popular political figure in the country at the time. He had the trust of both black and white. If only he had indicated that he really was in power and that his objective was change, he could have carried the day. But it became clear to us all that not only was he not really in control, he didn't have the necessary passion for social change. I have often wondered if inheriting power so quickly corrupted him. It seemed as if he was satisfied just with being Prime Minister, that this was achievement enough. He certainly wasn't on fire for his people.

He failed completely in the two things he most needed to do to prove that he really was head of government and that the blacks had tangible power – to end sanctions and to bring about a cease fire. Britain refused to recognise any settlement that didn't take the Patriotic Front into consideration and so she refused to recognise the Interim Government or to lift sanctions. Far from ending the war, the sacking of Byron Hove was a further insult to African hopes and added burning coals to the fire.

A stepping stone is never recognised for its importance, it's just stepped on. It's easy to write Muzorewa off as a complete sell-out, but the truth is that there was no way Rhodesia could have moved straight from Ian Smith to Robert Mugabe – there had to be a stage in between. Muzorewa as the first black the whites would trust, was that stepping stone. He was an essential part of the progress towards the new Zimbabwe. At the time, however, our thoughts towards him were less charitable.

Another result of the sacking was that Arthur got kicked out of the party. He'd begun to be a threat to Muzorewa because he felt the Bishop should be pushing to work with Nkomo and Mugabe, as well as my father, and this was not a welcome suggestion to a man who feared political rivals. When Byron Hove was sacked Arthur remonstrated with Muzorewa and this was the final straw in a relationship that had been growing steadily more tense. Arthur was turned out on his ear, but for him it was almost a relief. It liberated him to work with all sides and to try to bring them all together in a new peace initiative. He very nearly succeeded.

This period was a difficult one at home. I tried to explain to Dad what was going on and how seriously the sacking of Byron Hove had affected the confidence of the people. But Dad was in no mood to listen. Nothing I said seemed to get through to him. And he was, after all, playing his own game. He supported Bishop Muzorewa because he could see he was a weak man, and Dad's primary concern was to protect the interest of the white community. He felt fairly certain that under the Bishop nothing too radical would take place to materially alter the status quo.

It wasn't just Arthur who wanted all sides to get together. From all over the world the pressure came on the Interim Government to hold all party talks, but my Dad would not countenance Mugabe, whom I must say was regarded by most people as the arch terrorist. However he did have secret talks with Nkomo to try to persuade him to come back to Rhodesia and take a position in the government. But it was no go. Nkomo for once wouldn't budge without Mugabe. All hopes of even tentative talks with the Patriotic Front were finally shattered by the Viscount Massacre.

On September 3rd, Nkomo's forces, using a Russian made Sam 7 heat seeking missile, shot down a Rhodesian Viscount on a domestic flight from Kariba to Salisbury. Thirty-eight passengers and crew died in the crash, but eighteen survived. As they staggered through the bush, stunned and wounded, the guerillas picked them off, one by one, women and children. Only eight were left alive.

The whites were horrified. We listened with mounting distress as the hatred and desire for vengeance we had been working so hard to dispell came bubbling to the surface. Security Forces retaliated on the guerillas by attacking Nkomo's transit camp in Zambia. More than 300 people died and the casualties were reported to be over one and a half thousand.

The fighting went on with renewed ferocity. By the summer it was thought maybe as many as 10,000 blacks had joined the guerilla forces and the war was costing our country £500,000 a day.

Now the older men were being called up for national service — everyone under 50, and there were plans to conscript the blacks as well. In the rural areas controlled by the guerillas everyday life was falling to bits; taxes were not being paid; local councils were packing up; schools and missions were being forced to close; agricultural production was being seriously disrupted with fairly devastating effects and the veterinary services were so badly curtailed that half a million cattle died during the year — at a cost of about £30 million.

The guerillas began to concentrate on hitting schools and isolated white farmsteads and we saw the beginning of a new and ominous development. Some of the guerillas were deserting the main armies, or splitting off into factional groups. They formed private armies, intimidating rural blacks for their support and letting off steam in bursts of random violence. It was chaos.

Everyone was by now completely disillusioned by the Interim Government and we were not a bit surprised when Dad announced that there would not be majority rule by December 31st after all.

Our 'Cabinet of Conscience' met more frequently as the pressure mounted. We still believed God had another way for our country, but I'm sure there was a new anguish in many of our prayers. Arthur's mixed services continued and the grass roots movement grew, inspite of, or maybe because, many of us were now suffering personal losses among our families and friends.

21. Dying for the Truth

Arthur became haunted by the thought of the dying. He began to dream about the boys fighting in the bush. He loved them and he couldn't forget that in those early days he had sought them out and encouraged them to go. Now his one consuming desire was to find a way to end the war. He kept saying, over and over again, 'Our people have suffered enough. Our people have suffered enough.'

One day a group of us, black and white, had got together to pray and we were discussing fear. How do you keep free from fear in a situation like war? Fear warps your judgement. It paralyses you, so that you can't act for good, even if you want to.

Suddenly, in the middle of our discussion, Arthur announced quite out of the blue it seemed, that he had a plan. He was going to cross the borders into Zambia and Mozambique to see Nkomo and Mugabe and try to bring them together in a fresh peace bid.

We were stunned. The terrorist war was now extremely violent, the men desperate and determined. The thought of Arthur crossing the fighting lines for a friendly chat seemed ludicrously dangerous. And to what end?

'What can you say to them Arthur? What do you think you can achieve that no-one else has?'

But he was adamant. He felt God was telling him to bring these two men together and to draw them into peace negotiations with the Interim Government.

I remember him saying, 'How can you make your enemy your friend if you never meet him?' Somehow he felt he had to bring all these enemies together to discuss their common ground and to help them see that the people had suffered enough. I was as anxious for him as the rest.

'But Arthur, it will be so dangerous. The chances are you'll be killed before you're half way there. What good are you dead, man? That's not the answer.'

'Dear Brother Alec', he leaned towards me, his face alight with that smile of his, 'I'm not afraid to die. We've all got to die sometimes. What matters is what we are living for when death meets us.'

Over the next few days we all tried to talk him out of it, Hugh, Henry, and I, but he would not be dissuaded. God had told him to go, he said, and go he must.

News trickled back to us. Arthur went up to Lusaka and Byron Hove flew down from London to meet him. Together they met the leaders of Nkomo's men. They were more than glad to see them. The ZAPU leaders there had little contact with people who lived inside the country and were anxious for accurate news and information.

Meeting Mugabe was more dificult. First he sent his ablest lieutenant to vet Arthur in Lusaka and only when he had passed that test was he allowed into the presence of Simon Muzenda, Mugabe's close colleague, now the deputy Prime Minister.

The guerillas didn't give him an easy ride. Arthur was in his early 50s by this time, but still they wanted to see what he was made of. They marched him through the bush all night, expecting him to keep up with the trained soldiers and to suffer the rigours of their everyday life. He poured himself out to keep up with them, and all the time he talked of his feelings for the country and his vision for an end to the fighting. Finally he flew back to Salisbury, ill and exhausted, and was taken to hospital.

But for him it had been worth it. He sensed among the men a great weariness. They were all tired of fighting and disillusioned by the continual diplomatic deadlocks. They welcomed any serious advance to ending the war. Arthur was confident that he could work with them, but he knew that their trust in him endangered his own life. Both Muzorewa and my father's party would now be profoundly suspicious of him for having made such a foray into the enemy camp.

I went to see him several times while he was in hospital and it was clear that he felt an urgency to get his peace initiative moving. I remember him saying that he must get to see them both and tell them of the mood of the guerillas and the hopes he saw for a settlement.

'It'll be dangerous', I said, 'Dad'll see you, you know he will, but Muzorewa isn't feeling too friendly towards you at the moment. He's been attacking you on the radio this week. You've become highly suspect now.'

'I know'. Arthur chuckled, partly at the thought, and partly at my face which must have looked very concerned. 'Brother Alec', he said.

When he was better he did see my father. I wasn't in on their conversation but I know they parted with an understanding. Dad said he'd agreed with every word Arthur had spoken and had pledged him his support for the new peace plans. Since Dad had, up until that time, refused even to talk about Mugabe, that was really something.

And so, despite all our fears and warnings, Arthur had managed to win the confidence of three of our four warring leaders. No one had ever achieved that much before. We felt a new hope. Perhaps Arthur was going to make it, to bring together men who had previously refused to meet. If anyone had the faith and the charisma to unite the irreconcilable, it was Arthur, who in his own life had overcome so much bitterness for the sake of the common good. When the time was ripe, he would see Muzorewa.

It was by now mid December. Arthur came to see us late one evening as we were gathered together. As he walked through the door we were struck by a curious difference in him. His beard – the symbol of an African nationalist politician – was gone. My last memory is of him laughing at us.

'This year', he said, stroking his shiny new chin, 'I want to have a quiet Christmas and see what more I need to shed from my life to become more like Christ.'

The next day was December 18th. We heard later that two young blacks had come to the gates of his house and asked to see him.

'Dad, be careful', said his son, who didn't like the look of them. 'I'm not sure about those guys.'

'O come, come Noble', he smiled, and patting

him on the shoulder, walked towards the gates. Gladys, was watching from the door.

The young men asked Arthur to drive them to his church, we never knew on what pretext. Arthur took them in his car and was last seen driving towards town.

The next morning his car was found 50 kilometres from the city. His body, lying beside it, was riddled with bullets.

Arthur was prepared for death. For several months, since he began his new role as 'go-between', he felt his days to be numbered. He even said to us once, 'Every day that I have is by the grace of God.' When he told Gladys that he might shortly die, she was terribly distressed. He put his arm around her and held her close. 'Gladys, why are you weeping? I am going to die for the truth.'

But if he was prepared, we were not, and the shock was terrible. I felt shattered. I was so completely destroyed in my spirit and in my heart. I couldn't believe he was dead. He had meant so much to me personally, and so much to the country. He was our hope for peace and with his death, our hope died.

To me personally he gave trust and friendship. In my early days as a Christian he had helped me realise the power of Christ, and to channel my longing to serve. He gave me a new understanding of my country and a new vision. Even after his funeral I could not believe that he was really gone. I kept expecting to turn a corner and see him there, larger than life.

Tributes poured in to him from all over the world. His memorial service in Salisbury was packed out with blacks and whites from every station in life. In its editorial comment our leading paper, the

Rhodesian Herald, wrote; 'It is a tragedy that men of this calibre... who concern themselves so deeply with the welfare of their fellow citizens, should not live to see the completion of their work. Instead others must take up the burden... Surely there must be some with both the courage and conviction to inherit the mantle?'

Surely there must be some. But it was not us. It was not me. We were spent. We kept meeting together and talking about him to ease our grief, but grief is not so easily assuaged.

22. The Miracle of Peace

We limped through the next year unaware that although Arthur was dead, his influence among world politicians was very much alive. We saw Bishop Muzorewa finally voted in as our first black Prime Minister over a constitution which still kept the control of the police, army, judiciary and the civil service in white hands. The UN declared the elections null and void even before they took place and the fighting got worse.

It was then that Mrs. Thatcher, the newly elected British Prime Minister, made her only known U-turn. She was all set to recognise the Muzorewa government, encouraged by her right wing advisors, when Lord Carrington persuaded her to give him one more chance in trying to bring about a fairer settlement involving the Patriotic Front. She agreed to hold an all-party constitutional conference at Lancaster House in London.

The world press followed these tortuous 14 weeks when Bishop Muzorewa, my father, Mugabe and Nkomo fought and argued and struggled their way to eventual agreement. There were times when the problems seemed absolutely insurmountable. Lord Carrington steered his way through minefield after minefield and many unofficial talks went on behind the scenes — initiated by Christians — to encourage the delegates to settle.

So on 21st December 1979, exactly seven years to the day after the start of the guerilla war, the Lancaster House Agreement was signed. There was to be an immediate cease fire; the guerillas and security forces were to disengage, the government was to grant an amnesty to nationalist exiles and fighters and the Patriotic Front was to be declared a legal party, authorised to campaign in the coming election. This time true independence was in sight.

The general feeling among the whites was one of resignation tempered by tiredness. Everyone was sick of war. Some whites had been in and out of the army for years. Their lives had been turned upside down and their spirits sickened by the carnage. They all knew there was no way they could win and so they accepted the reality of black majority rule and waited to see what the outcome of the elections would be.

It could have been mayhem. Lord Soames was appointed Governor and flew out before fighting had properly ceased to supervise it all. When Nkomo and Mugabe eventually returned there were huge rallies to meet them which we all expected to erupt. Mugabe's initial manifesto was very radical and anti-white. He was rumoured to have a hit list of men he wanted to assassinate — at the top of the list was Dad, of course. He said he was going to close all the churches and use them as social centres. He publically stated what we all knew and feared, that he was a Marxist-Lenninist and intended to turn Rhodesia into a socialist state. The whites had better watch out.

Meanwhile, even though a cease fire had been called, bombs were still going off amid sporadic fighting. There were tales of intimidation and brutality by all parties and several assassination attempts were made on Mugabe. Dad was touring the country calling him 'The Red Terror' and many of the administrators thought the elections just wouldn't come off at all and the whole thing would blow up in our faces.

There was plenty of conjecture, of course, but most people reckoned that Joshua Nkomo would come out on top. It didn't occur to most of us that Mugabe might. He was regarded by most whites as so extreme and violent a man as to be hardly human – an image the Rhodesian Front had lovingly fostered – and it was quite simply unthinkable that he should ever become PM.

Whoever won the election, we feared trouble, and that's when the army planned their coup. General Walls, their Commander-in-Chief, was the master mind and he had all vital installations surrounded. The assembly points for the elections were manned only by territorials so that all the regulars could be deployed for the coup. Armoured tanks were parked conspicuously in the side streets of the capital.

The coup was the white's contingency plan against two possibilities; they were afraid that whoever got in there would be massive civil disturbances with Dad being strung up by his neck in Cecil Square and mass killings of whites. They also wanted to make quite sure that they could crush Mugabe in the unlikely eventuality of his getting elected. And it was considered unlikely.

Our own intelligence service and the Russian intelligence service had put their money on Joshua Nkomo. There was little doubt in our minds that he would be the next Prime Minister.

As the results of polling began to roll in it became clear to those running the election that the thing the whites dreaded most was going to happen. Lord Soames moved fast. He alone saw the true nature of Mugabe's victory. He saw that it was going to be overwhelmingly popular, that despite initial difficulties, it had been a fair and free election. The second vital thing Lord Soames realised was that Mugabe's victory was a smack in the eye for Russia. Mugabe detested the Russians and his election turned out to be the biggest set back for Soviet foreign policy in Africa for 20 years or more. Russia had backed Nkomo, he was their man, and they'd been quietly confident of victory. So it was clear that if the whites launched a coup against Mugabe, the people's choice, then they would actually be doing themselves more harm than good. They would be opening the door to continuing bloodshed and increasing the possibility of Russian interference. General Walls was persuaded to disperse his troups and the armoured vehicles trundled quietly away.

In his Independence Day speech Mugabe was to say of Lord Soames; 'He is indeed a great man ... I shall certainly be missing a good friend and counsellor.'

Many people involved in Rhodesia during those days think the peaceful outcome of the elections a miracle. Lord Soames himself described it as such. Yet there was another meeting, another miracle, which nobody knew about at the time.

Observers felt afterwards that this secret meeting was a crucial step in calming white fears and averting the expected bloodbath. It came about, as so much action did at that time, from prayer.

Once it became clear that Mugabe was going to win, and the rumours of a coup began to circulate, our anxiety for the country's future became acute. We called a hasty meeting of the 'Cabinet of Conscience' and began to pray, asking God what we should be doing. We felt a rising hopelessness as our country appeared to be heading for another awful crisis and I think many of us cried out to God in despair.

One of the men with us was called Joram, and he'd been connected with Mugabe's party for some while. As we sat in silence, waiting upon God, he felt convinced that we should get Mugabe and my father together. He knew that the one thing they had in common was love for their country and a longing to rebuild it in peace – enough, he felt, to provide a starting point for understanding. He was sure that if they could only find a level of acceptance for each other, the nation would be calmed.

I must say the rest of us thought the whole idea quite crazy considering the hatred the two of them had expressed for one another. But Joram was convinced that we should at least try. He went away to work on Mugabe and I went to work on Dad. It took a long time and several meetings. They both consulted their advisors and the days ticked by. It began to look as though the whole idea would fall through.

Whether it was the sudden presence of armoured cars or not, I don't know, but at the eleventh hour – the night before Mugabe was to be announced victor – he rang Joram to say he was ready to meet Dad, if Dad would meet him. The meeting was to take place after dark and in Mugabe's own house.

Dad insisted on going alone. When he arrived Jorum opened the door to him. There were only three other people present, Mr. Mugabe and two of his senior colleagues.

When Jorum told me about it all afterwards he couldn't help laughing – it was the sheer improbability of it all. The Central Committee of the Patriotic Front had contingency plans to leave the country in the event of trouble; the whites had their coup all lined up and ready to go; Mugabe was unable to leave his house because of the attempts on his life and in through the front door of this arch terrorist's home walks the man on the top of his hit list, Ian Smith. And what happened? Piecing together the story from Dad and Jorum afterwards I gather the two shook hands, and Mugabe suggested he got the ball rolling by explaining his policies for the new Zimbabwe and the way he hoped to lead the country. The two men became completely absorbed in each other and the rest of the party just faded into the woodwork.

Dad said he was totally convinced of Mugabe's desire for reconciliation. The aggressive stance of his early manifesto had mellowed as he realised that retaliation would only continue to destroy. He had also changed his mind about closing the churches when he realised how deeply spiritual his own people were. I've often thought there was a lot of confusion in the minds of the Patriotic Front in the early days because, after all, they too had been subjected to fairly relentless propaganda and they all have to sift out the wheat from the chaff when they got home – Mugabe included.

Anyway he and Dad discussed many areas of policy and thrashed out the white contribution to the new cabinet and what role, if any, Dad himself would play. The two of them clearly found an unexpected respect for one another. Jorum was right.

In the end Mugabe promised that there would be no recriminations on the whites and for his part Dad promised to try to persuade them to calm down and to give Mugabe their support. The next day he made a public broadcast which must have astounded the nation. He urged his 'fellow whites' to stay and to give the new regime a chance. His obvious trust in Mugabe's goodwill did a lot to diffuse the tension. I don't expect the Europeans had ever expected to hear him say anything so constructive about the man he once dubbed 'The Red Terror'.

That evening we all heard, in public form, what Mr Mugabe had promised to Dad in private. It's hard to understand, but most of us had never even seen Mugabe. His picture never appeared in the newspapers. We had no idea of what he looked like, or how he spoke. We had been taught to regard him as a monster. When he appeared that night on television to announce the independence of Zimbabwe to the nation, many whites were taken off guard by this cultured, well spoken and highly articulate man who was now their Prime Minister. For myself, there are parts of his speech I shall never forget. In fact I went out the next day to buy copies of it. I'd not heard finer preaching from the pulpit!

'Tomorrow', he had said, 'we are being born again; born again not as individuals, but collectively as a people, as a viable nation of Zimbabweans . . .

'Tomorrow we shall cease to be men and women

119

of the past and become men and women of the future. It's tomorrow then, not yesterday, which bears our destiny . . .

'Our new nation requires of everyone of us to be a new man, with a new mind, a new heart and a new spirit.

'Our new mind must have a new vision and our new hearts a new love that spurns hate and a new spirit that must unite and not divide . . .

'Henceforth you and I must strive to adapt ourselves, intellectually and spiritually to the reality of our political change and relate to each other as brothers bound one to another by a bond of national comradeship . . .

'The wrongs of the past must now stand forgiven and forgotten.'

There are always problems with emerging nations, but in the years since Prime Minister Mugabe made that statement, I have found his sentiments reiterated time and time again by the black Africans I've worked among. The world press is quick to pounce on situations that might not be working as they should, but very slow to point out the countless instances of reconciliation in public and private life that take place every day.

23. The Killing Machines

Our attitude to miracles has been too much influenced by Hollywood. We think a miracle has to include the voice of God roaring through clouds and thunder, or an old fellow in a dirty coat wacking the sea with a big stick. But God's miracles are often very quiet. It takes a wise man to see them, but they're miracles nevertheless. And for my money, what happened in the army after Independence was just such a miracle.

Take a young man who, in normal circumstances, leaves school at 18 and goes to university. In three years he might get a bachelor's degree. In another two years a masters. He may go on, two years later, to get a PhD. So in seven years he would have become an expert in his field.

Now in 1972, when war broke out, that same young man might have joined the army. By 1979, when the peace agreement was signed he had, in effect, a PhD in the art of hating and killing. He would not have learnt his trade any less thoroughly than a doctor or an engineer. In fact he'd probably have learnt it better because the sort of decisions he was making meant the difference between his living and dying.

By 1979 there were some men who had been in the army for 10 or 20 years. They were highly trained killing machines and everything they had been taught over the last decade or so reinforced their views that Mugabe was their enemy, that Mugabe's forces were communist terrorists and a threat to decent society. They were taught that to kill them was to do good, was to do right. To hate them was an acceptable emotion.

Now, all of a sudden, we were patting these men on the back and saying, 'Thanks. You've done a good job, but it's all over now. Shake hands and be friends. Yesterday Mugabe was your enemy, today he's your Prime Minister. Yesterday you would have been a hero to shoot and kill him, today you've got to salute and obey him'.

To expect men to take such a leap of the imagination was impossible, yet that's just what we were asking them to do because one of the most urgent tasks after Independence was to integrate the three armies – the two guerilla forces, ZANLA and ZIPRA, and the white Rhodesian army – into one coherent unit. Without their integration there would be no real peace in the land.

Working with Arthur had given me a small insight into the nationalist mind. I felt I had caught a glimpse of their dreams and aspirations and of the hates and hurts that had caused the war. My involvement in the army, on the other hand, had given me an understanding of the white Rhodesian's state of mind. In a sense I have been privileged to mix with both sides and I felt I should offer my services, such as they were, to help in this task of army reconciliation.

I was accepted into the Corp of Chaplains, even though I wasn't ordained, shortly before Independence was declared, and with my new colleagues set about trying to find ways of tackling this seemingly insoluble problem.

The army by this time was huge – about 80-90 thousand men – and to begin with each of us worked in separate battalions trying to establish one-to-one relationships with as many men as possible and developing compulsory weekly meetings.

During the first year our task was to de-politicize the soldiers. We had to help them to accept the results of the election and to face up to the new political situation. For whites it was particularly hard to grasp. They had really been quite ignorant about the causes of the civil war. It's so easy to be brainwashed, to have only half the truth, especially when the press is as much under the thumb of the government as ours was under the Rhodesian Front. The opposition paper had been banned and our school history lessons certainly didn't reveal the truth about our forebears attitudes and actions towards the Africans. This process of re-education was quite an eye-opener to many white soldiers, and a painful process of reassessment.

We also had to try to detune their killing instincts and to re-orientate them so that they would be able to settle into civilian life. Imagine what it was like, especially for the blacks. Most of them had come as young men from nothing – from poverty, unemployment and hopelessness – into a movement that had given them a purpose and a status. But their only training was to kill.

They were outlaws to society and had never been under the social restrictions of normal everyday life. We couldn't just confine men like that to a tiny office and tell them to get on with civilian life. It didn't make sense. The readjustments they had to face were too great.

So we had to encourage and develop in all the men a new social conscience based on a multi-racial society that had, according to the Prime Minister, to forgive and forget the past. It was a complete about face for the Africans who had spent years feeding off the hatred a memory of the past had given them.

The whites, on the other hand, had to realise that the men they had always regarded as servants were brothers; that the guerillas they had been taught to despise had been fighting for a just cause and that from now on all privilege was to be shared.

In the second year of peace our aim was to try to integrate the different forces, ZANLA, ZIPRA and the Rhodesian army, into one unit. Our success here was only partial, partly because there were so few of us and so many of them, and partly because what we were asking of them was so momentous. Many white soldiers left to join the South African Army and ZIPRA soldiers – Nkomo's men – left to become dissidents – the very thing we were trying to avoid.

But even so, as far as I was concerned, we were living in miracle alley. That even one soldier could be reconciled with his enemy was amazing, that thousands were reconciled is a wonder. Many people wave an airy hand and say, 'Of course we've got an integrated army now' without even vaguely understanding what individual people had to go through in terms of personal re-orientation to achieve that unity.

24. The Christian Challenge

Mr. Mugabe's Independence speech should have roused every Christian heart in the land. The whole tone of his talk was so Christian in content that every believer's heart should have been warmed by the thought that he was talking our language. Christian leaders should have said, straight away and in public, that they were right behind him. I think if we had seized the initiative then, we could have been in the forefront of the government's thinking for the creation of a new society.

As it was, many of the country's most prominent Christians threw up their hands in horror crying,

'The Marxists are coming'. They fell over themselves in the rush to South Africa and there was a stampede of ministers who all of a sudden felt a call to preach in Cape Town or Papua, New Guinea.

By running away I think they did two very great wrongs. They poisoned the minds of the people to whom they fled. You have to justify an action like running away and I think they created an exaggerated and false picture of the reality of the situation here. You get far more sympathy by crying 'Terrible . . . Marxist State . . . only just escaped in time', than if you give the real reason for your leaving – that you didn't have the courage to battle it out.

An even worse consequence, perhaps, was that by going they gave Christianity a bad name. Christians should be people that others look to for inspiration, for leadership, for strength, but the example they set was of cowardice and self interest.

Having said that, there were of course many Christians who stayed. They are doing invaluable work and they are meant, I believe, to form the hard core of those who will help pull Zimbabwe through. Unfortunately, they are not the ones who get the publicity.

The thing that has struck me about that Independence speech, and that has impressed me since, is that neither Mugabe nor his government – apart from three or four perhaps – are doctrinaire Marxists. They are nationalists searching for an ideology that is suitable for this country. Marxist-Leninism is an alien concept to the African because atheism is alien. Mugabe himself was brought up a Catholic and has since described his political beliefs as 'Christian Marxism'. He has an admitted sympathy to spiritual matters.

Such a sympathy opens the door to Christians in our country. It's clear that the government are trying to create an indiginous African system suitable to our people and our heritage. They are trying to work out a new way, and we should be alongside them. If Africa is looking for a new social order we, as Christians, should be the living proof that Christianity is the true socialism, that Christianity is a viable and better alternative to Marxism. But who is there to tell them about the possibilities of God's revolution when the Christians flee like lemmings leaving Christ with no voice in the land? Christians shouldn't be on retreat. They should be aflame for God and now is the time to act, while our country is still in the balance.

If you look at the structures of African life you will see that the Africans are instinctively socialist. They are a spiritual people and the willingness to forgive is an inherent part of African nature.

When Independence came to Zimbabwe, so did peace. Within a few weeks roads that had been too dangerous for whites to drive along, even in broad daylight, were quiet and safe. The country was restored to normality remarkably quickly and the incidents of retaliation were very few when you consider the length and bitterness of the war. We now have the former guerilla leader heading a government that contains and includes the man he rose up to depose. My father's deputy, David Smith, was until recently in Mugabe's cabinet and the Minister of Agriculture is also a white man. Where else in the world can you find such an outcome to 'revolution'? This willingness to forgive should give us hope that, despite our problems, Zimbabwe can be made to work. It must be made to work if we, and the rest of Southern Africa, are not to go up in flames.

Both the Soviet Union and South Africa, for different reasons, would like to see Zimbabwe collapse in confusion. If the Russians are able to move in and dominate our key country, it will not only affect all the neighbouring states, it will be the end of all the things we hold dear; religious freedom, individual freedom, human rights, equality before the law – all these ideals would be swept away.

If Zimbabwe is to succeed, then the whites must stay and the West should support us. The whites must stay to work alongside the government. As I know for myself, it means a total commitment on our part. It also means that the rest of the world should stop treating us like white expatriates. We are not expatriates – we're Africans and Africa is our only home.

In this country we see wealth and power side by side, and one of our important tasks is to close the gap between rich and poor. That may involve us in taking jobs in the public sector at lower wages, and being prepared to use our experience and advantages to develop other people's lives instead of maintaining the exceptional standards of our own. We have to work with the government in finding effective ways of redistributing the country's wealth and developing its very considerable natural resources.

We can't survive in isolation. We badly need the support of the Western world if Zimbabwe is to get off the ground.

It has been said that Zimbabwe is like a train just coming up to the points. It could go one way or the other, depending whose hand is on the lever. This is the hour of opportunity for men with a Christian answer. The whole world, not just Africa, is stuck for a way to bring races together, to heal hate, to share wealth among rich and poor. Where is there an answer, other than in the wisdom of God and the changing of men? Marxists believe that if you first change the structure of society, then a new kind of person will emerge. Christians believe that you need to change the person first, and then a new kind of society will emerge.

I believe that the hope for Zimbabwe doesn't just lie in a political system, or with a specific government, it lies in the people, black and white, who have come through the crisis and have changed. The Prime Minister was right when he made that speech — we do need new minds, new hearts and new spirits hewn, as they have been, from pain and humiliation, from repentance and forgiveness.